PICTURESQUE
CALIFORNIA HOMES

Samuel & Joseph C. Newsom.
Architects.

Reprinted from
Picturesque California Homes
No. 2. circa 1890
by
Samuel and Joseph Newsom, architects

Merrymeeting Archives, LLC © 2016
www.thevictorianhouse.com
ISBN 978-1-942745-06-8

Please consult your architect
for construction blueprints,
safety codes, and local regulations.

LOS ANGELES.

Front Elevation

Scale = 4 ft to one Inch

Samuel & Jos C Newsom
architects
604 Kearny St
S. F.

Parlor Finish

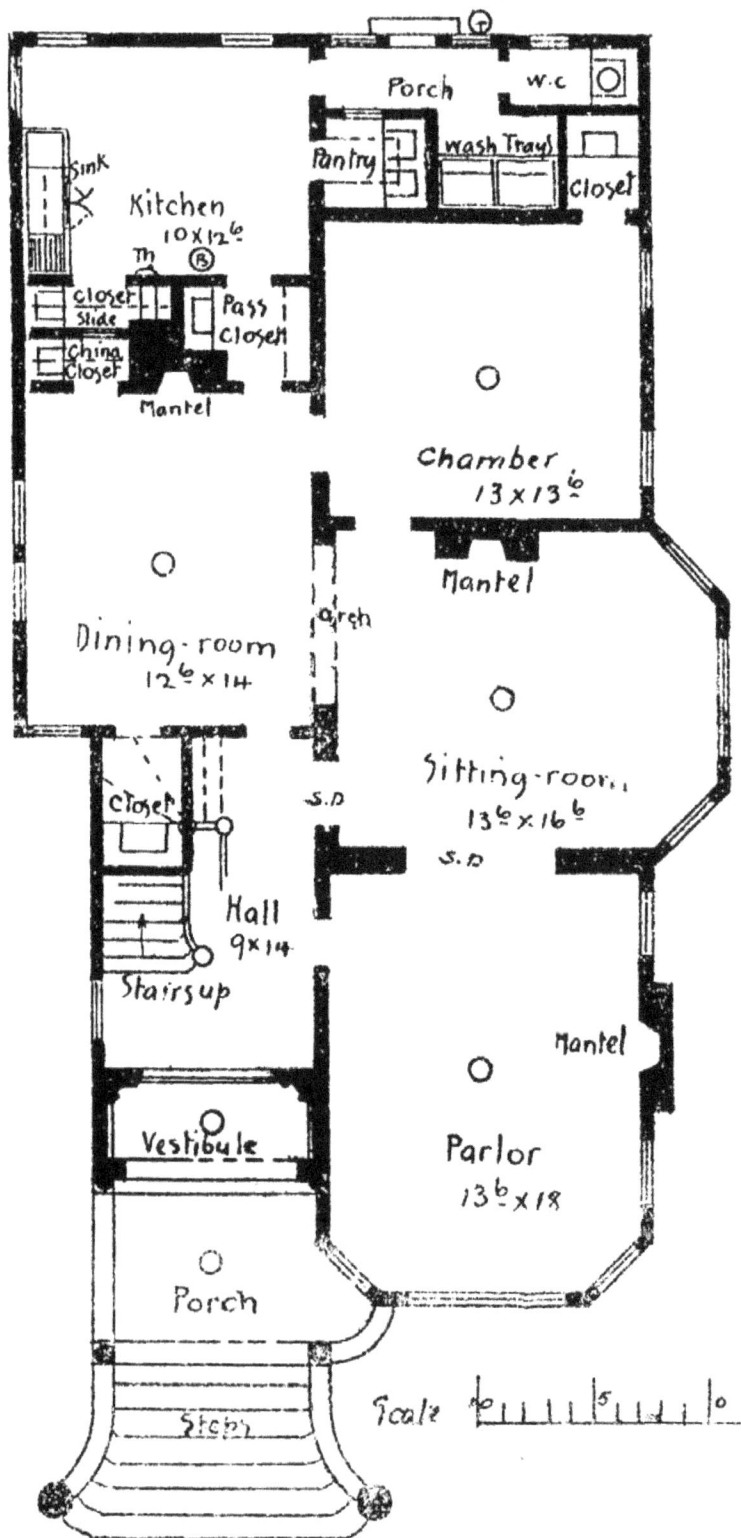

Porch

W.C

Sink

Pantry

Wash Trays

Closet

Kitchen
10×12⁶

Th

B

Closet
Slide

Pass
Closet

China
Closet

Mantel

Chamber
13×13⁶

Mantel

Dining-room
12⁶×14

arch

Closet

S.D

Sitting-room
13⁶×16⁶

S.D

Hall
9×14

Stairs up

Mantel

Vestibule

Parlor
13⁶×18

Porch

Scale

Steps

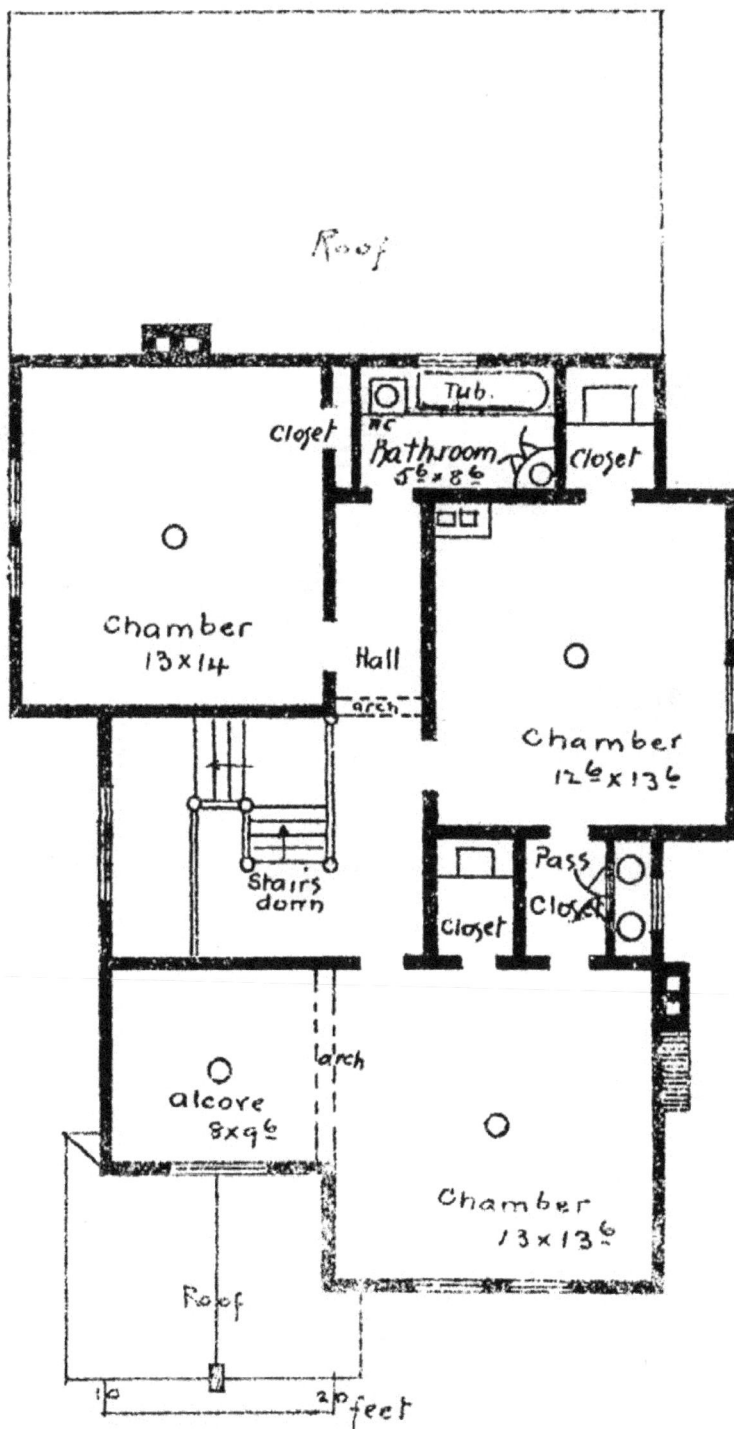

Roof

Closet

Tub.

#C

Bathroom
5⁶×8⁶

Closet

Chamber
13×14

Hall

arch

Chamber
12⁶×13⁶

Stairs
down

Pass

Closet

Closet

alcove
8×9⁶

arch

Chamber
13×13⁶

Roof

1⁰   2⁰ feet

LAKE-TAHOE.

A Rural Home of 8 rooms and large Entrance Hall.
Picturesque Exterior, Principal features
are the Outside Chimney, Tower, Corner Bays, Front
Horse Shoe Porch and Sweeping Steps and wooden
Mantels. The Building being square can be built
at a low Cost.

Front Elevation

~o Cost o~

Lumber	$ 800
Millwork Doors, Sash &c }	800
Labor	650
Plastering	175
Plumbing. Gas Fitting & Tinning }	175
Mantels	80
Brickwork & Drains	250
Bells &c	25
Hardware Nails &c	100
Painting	150

Total Cost $3205~

SCREEN

PANTRY

PORCH

DOWN

28"×73

3×78
20 7A.

W.C.

4G.4.
24"×78

B.T.

W.C.

BATH-
ROOM
75"×75

SINK

G
KITCHEN
11'3"×14'6"

UP

3.78

RANGE

3.75

G
CHAMBER

3.78

HALL
4'0"×10'0"

3.75

24"×78
CHINA CLOSET

24"×78

PASS
CLOSET

ARCH

LINEN
CLOSET 25"×75

20"×78

G
CHAMBER
12'8"×13'5"

1.8

HALL
5'6"×18'0"

47"×78

SHADE

1.8

DINING-ROOM
14'0"×18'5"

4'×78
C
S

24"×78
CLOSET

T.M.

24"×78
S.R.

PASS-
CLOSET

1.8

CLOSET

H.B.
52"×108
6'3"×10'9"

S.R.
G.R.

28"×95

S.R.
28"×78

C
S
4'6"×75

55"×10"
C
S

HALL
8'5"×12'5"

CHAMBER
135"×143

PARLOR
135"×18'2"

7A
56"×75

ARCH

VESTIBULE
ARCH

CATH.GLASS

H.B.

3 OUNCE GLASS
SHADE

1.8

GALLERY

1.8

SHADE
26 OUNCE GLASS

10(3)

PORCH

STEPS

SCALE 1 INCH=4 FEET

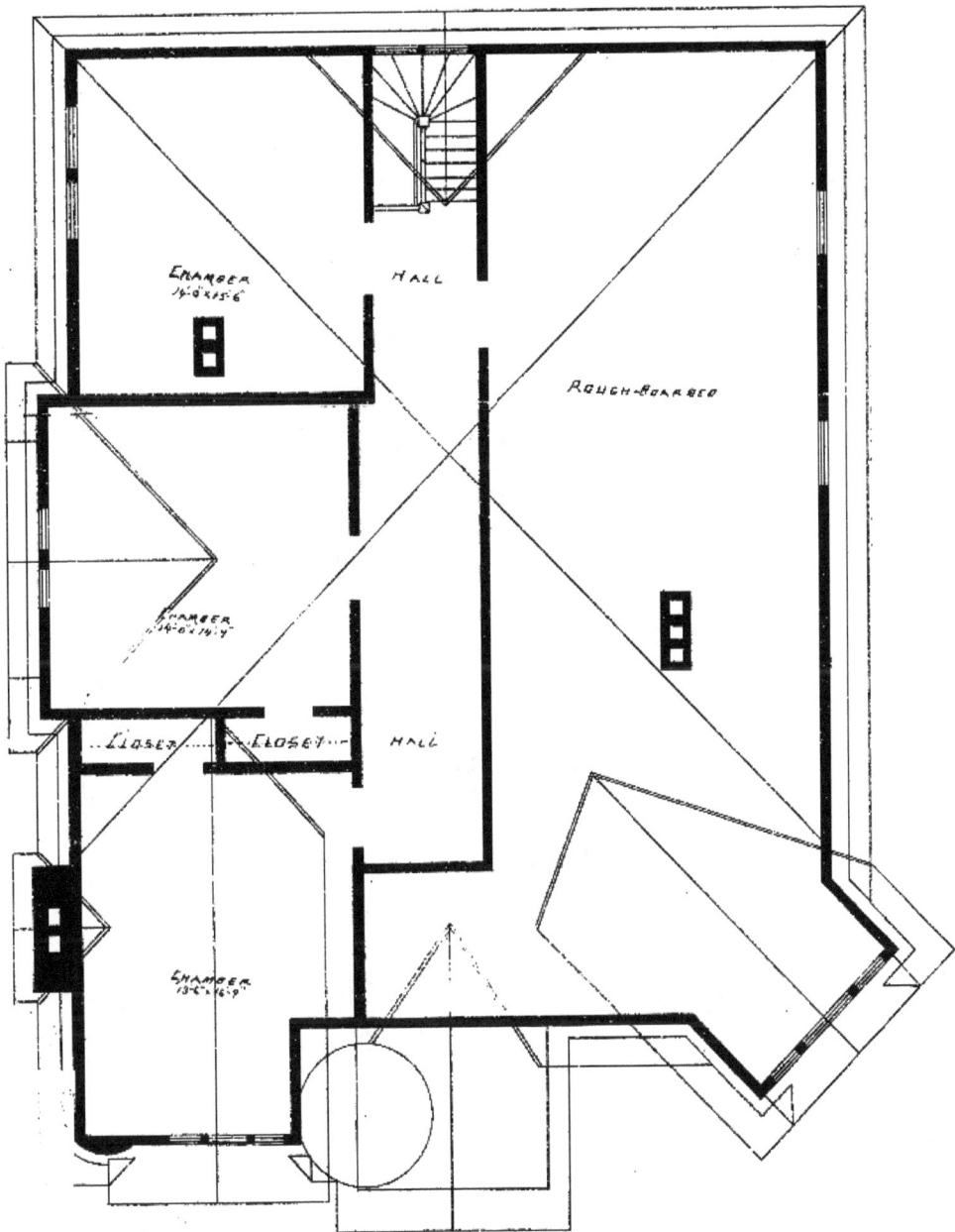

CHAMBER
16'-0"x15'-6"

HALL

ROUGH-BOARDED

CHAMBER
16'-0"x14'-4"

CLOSET   CLOSET   HALL

CHAMBER
13'-6"x16'-9"

PERALTA HEIGHTS.

Front Elevation.

Description.

A real Home for a small sum of Money. Staircase to be in Red-wood. The Den in front can be used for a Library or to receive visitors on business. The Dining-room has an Alcove off one end and large Bay on the other, the Parlor is connected with Sliding doors, which could be hung with curtains. Washtubs off Porch in rear and Laundry & Servants room is next to Kitchen. Up Stairs are 3 large rooms, all sunny, and convenient with large Pass Closet and basin. Bath room is in rear of the Hall. Stair-case Windows are in stained glass.

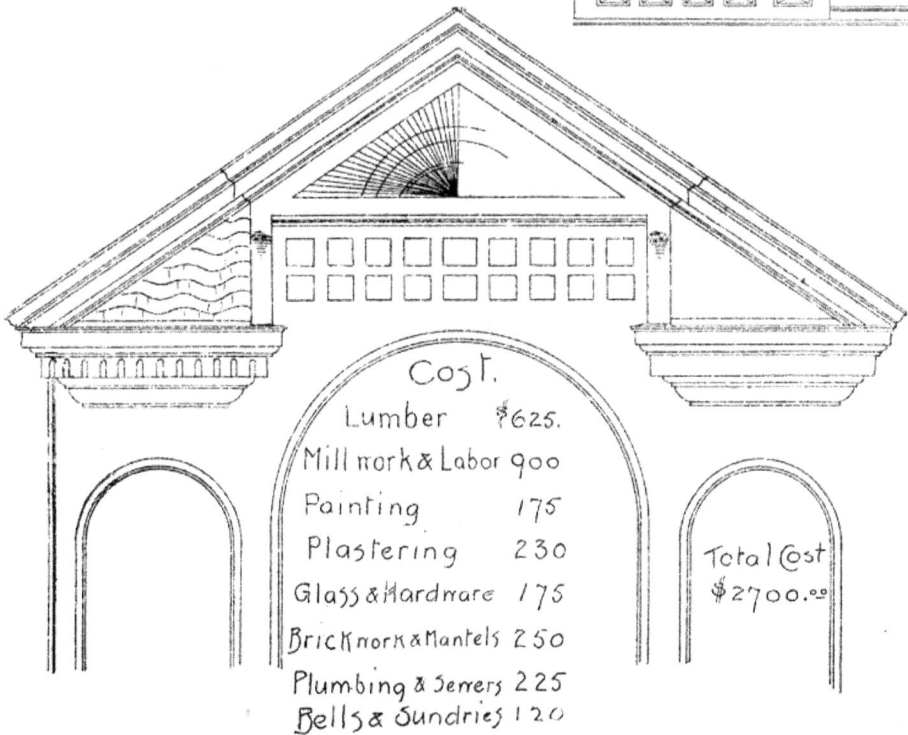

Cost.

Lumber	$625.
Mill work & Labor	900
Painting	175
Plastering	230
Glass & Hardware	175
Brickwork & Mantels	250
Plumbing & Sewers	225
Bells & Sundries	120

Total Cost $2700.00

coal & Wood Bins

S.H 4'8"

Porch

Stairs down

(G)

Servants-room
7' x 10'6"

Sink

(G)

(G)

Pass Closet

Kitchen
11' x 13

Boiler

ash flue

Mantel

(G)

arch

China Closet

(G)

(G)

Basin

Platform

Staircase Hall

Dining-room
13' x 16'

arch

Stairs up

Sliding doors

(G)

(G)

(G)

ash flue

Mantel

(G)

Hall

Den
7' x 10'

Vestibule
(G)

Parlor
12'6" x 15'

Bay
4' x 2'

Porch

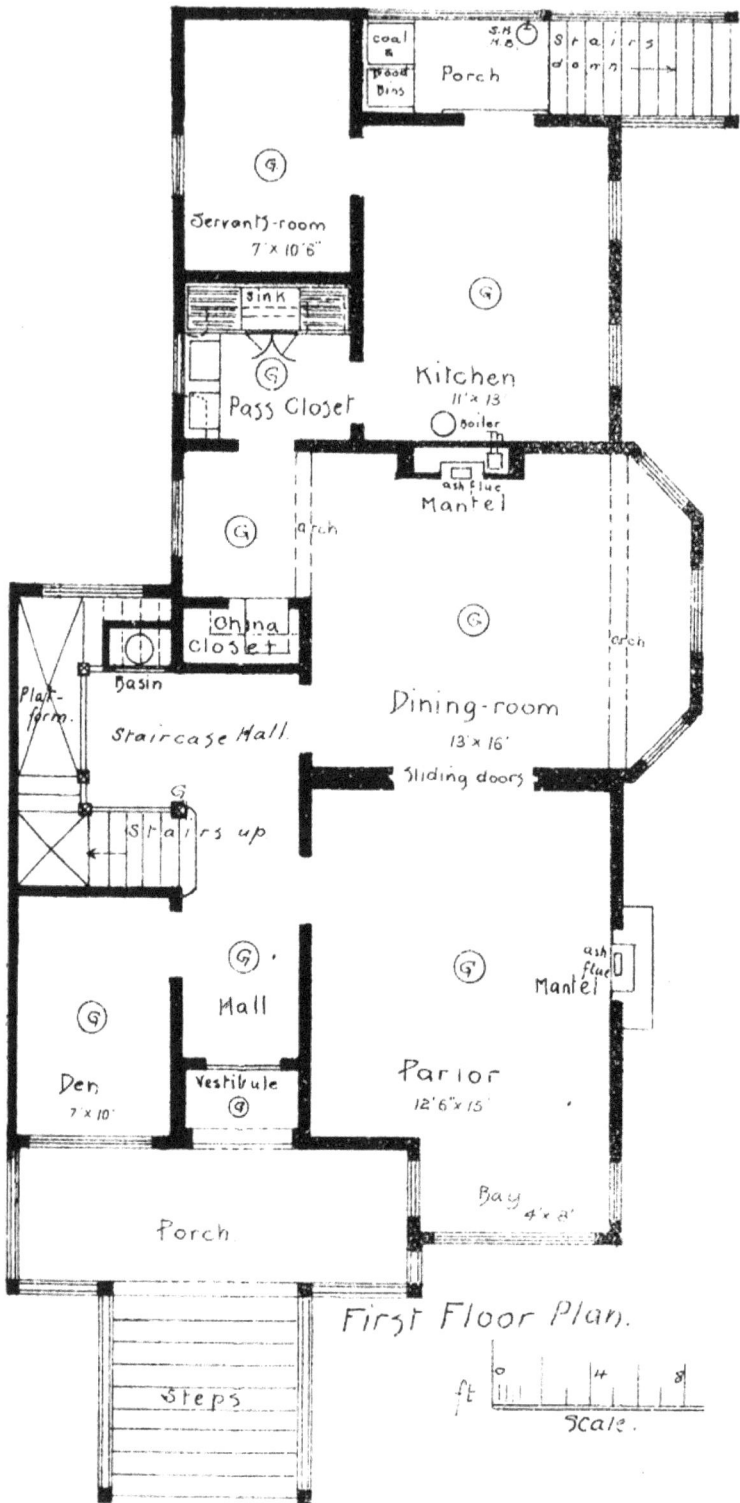

First Floor Plan.

ft   0   4   8

Scale.

Steps

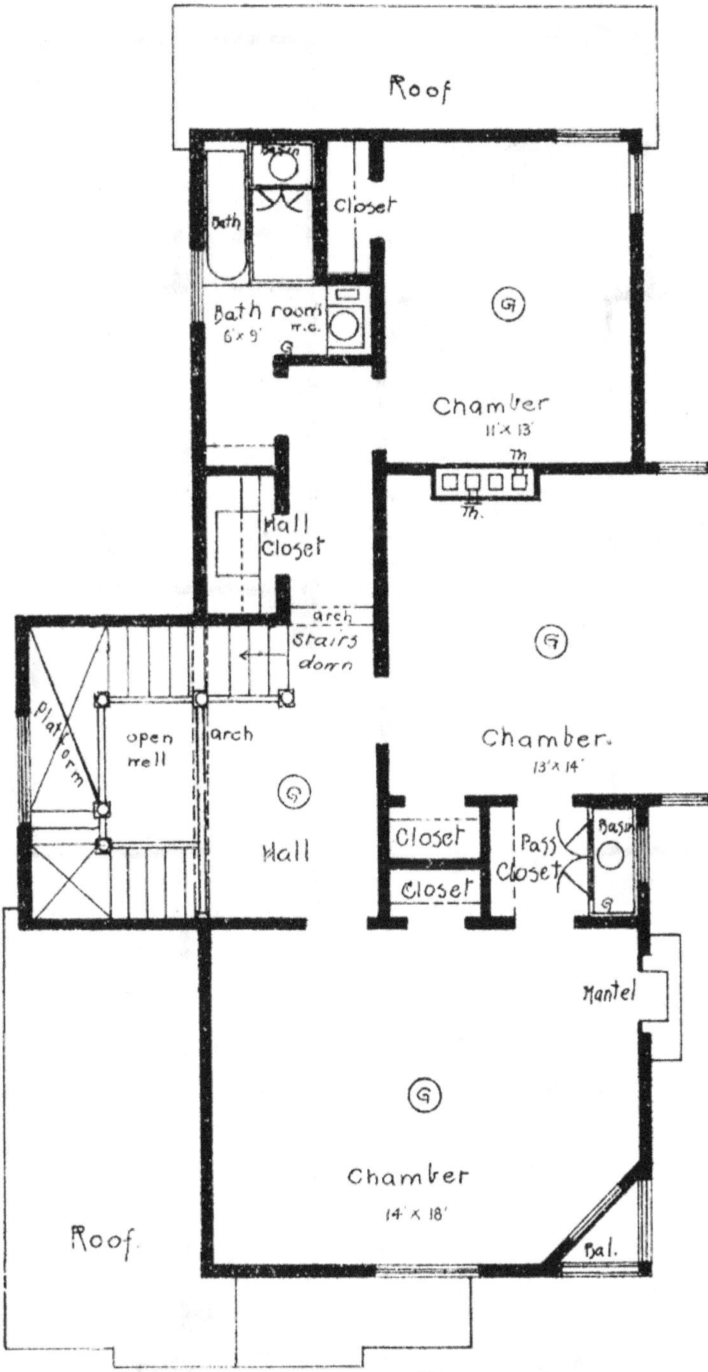

Roof

Basin

Bath

closet

Bath room
6' x 9'
w.c.

G

Chamber
11' x 13'

Th.

Th.

Hall
Closet

arch
Stairs
down

Platform

open
well

arch

G

Hall

G

Chamber
13' x 14'

Closet

Pass
Closet

Basin
9

Closet

Mantel

G

Chamber
14' x 18'

Bal.

Roof

Second Floor Plan

ft 0   4   8   12 ft.
Scale.

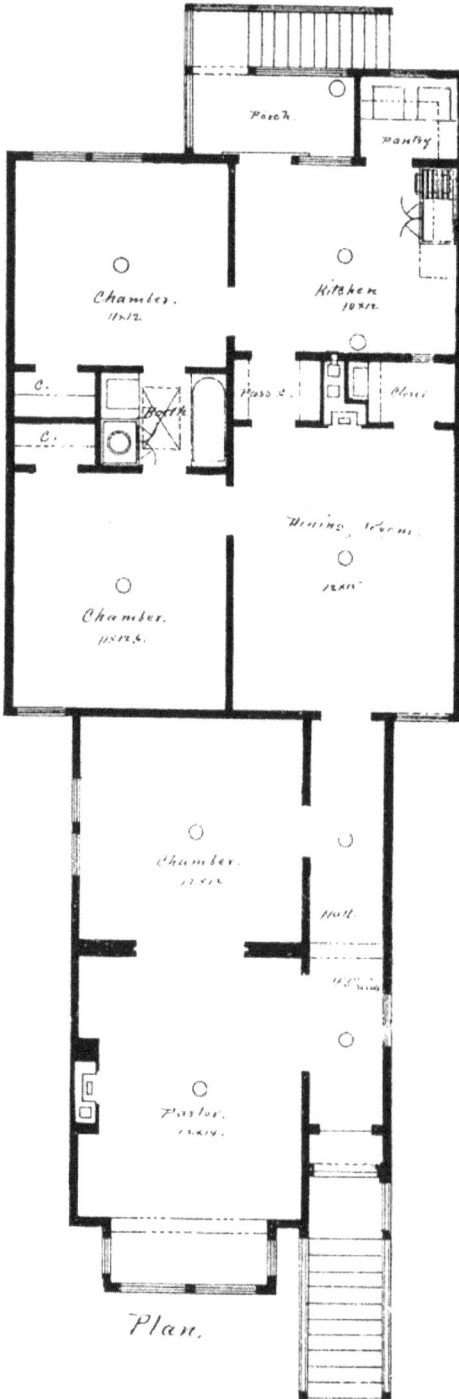

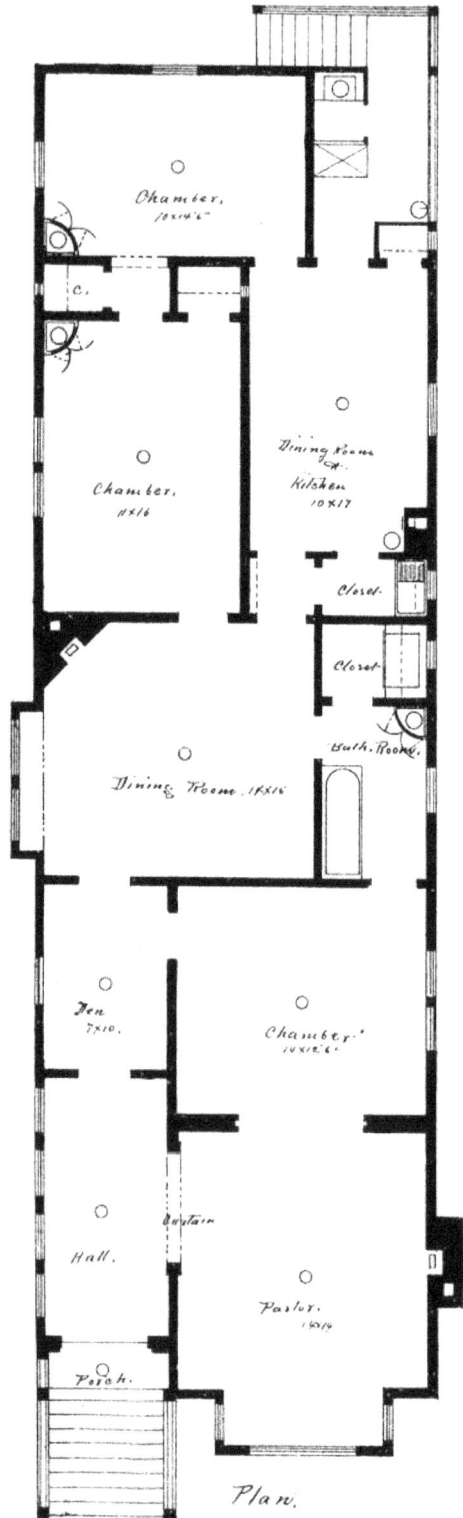

ST-HELENA

Chamber.
11×12

Kitchen.
10×12

Porch.

Pantry

C.

Bath

C.

Pass.

Closet

Dining Room.
12×11

Chamber.
11×12.6

Chamber.
12×12

Hall.

Parlor.
13×14

Plan.

Chamber.
10×14.6

C.

Dining Room.

Chamber.
11×16

Kitchen.
10×12

Closet.

Closet.

Bath Room.

Dining Room. 18×16

Den.
7×10.

Chamber.
10×12.6

Hall.

Upstair.

Parlor.
15×14

Porch.

Plan.

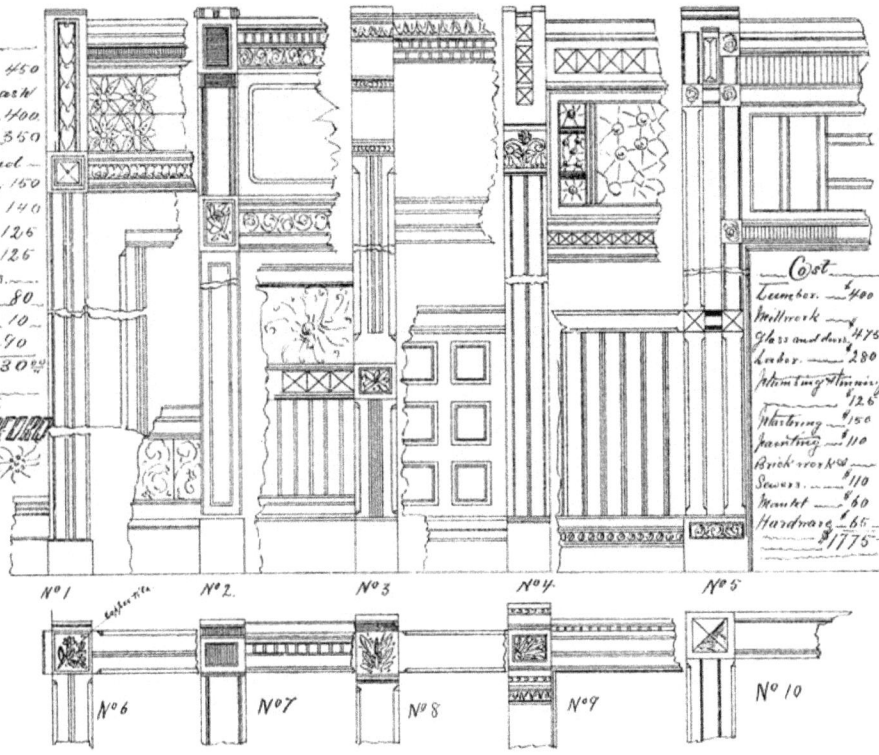

Cost.
Lumber 450
Mill work sash
doors &c. 400
Labor 350
Tinning and
plumbing 150
Plastering 140
painting 125
Brickwork 125
and Sewers
Mantel 80
Bells 10
Hardware 70
Total 1930⁰⁰

RUTHERFORD

Cost.
Lumber $400
Millwork
Glass and doors $475
Labor $280
plumbing & tinning
$125
Whitening $150
painting $110
Brick work $40
Sewers $110
Mantel $60
Hardware $65
$1775

Nº 1   Nº 2   Nº 3   Nº 4   Nº 5

Nº 6   Nº 7   Nº 8   Nº 9   Nº 10

Elevation.

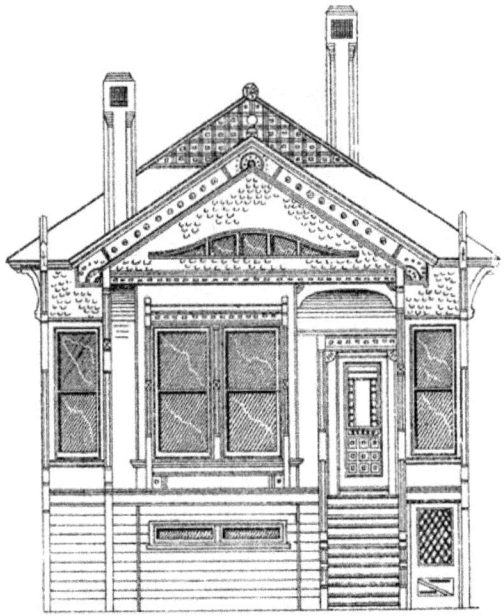

ELEVATION

Scale   5   10   20 ft

RIVERSIDE.

A Model Cottage with 8 rooms on one floor and 2 or more in attic. The Dining-room as a flower Bay window. The Parlor and Sitting room are connected by Sliding doors and off this is a Bed-room. The finish of this house is White Cedar - painted 5 coats of White and Gilded Mantels the same with Persian Tiles. The Den is finished in California Redwood, natural wood. Kitchen in Pine, natural wood, polished. All the floors are to be left in the natural wood polished

Estimated Cost	
Lumber	$650.00
Millwork. Glass. doors. Sash & Stairs	}1000.00
Painting	200.00
Plastering	350.00
Plumbing &c.	350.00
Hardware	150.00
Labor	700.00
Brick & Sewers	300.00
	$3700.00

Front Elevation

Samuel & Joseph C. NEWSOM
Architects
504 Kearny St
Top Floor
San Francisco. Cal.

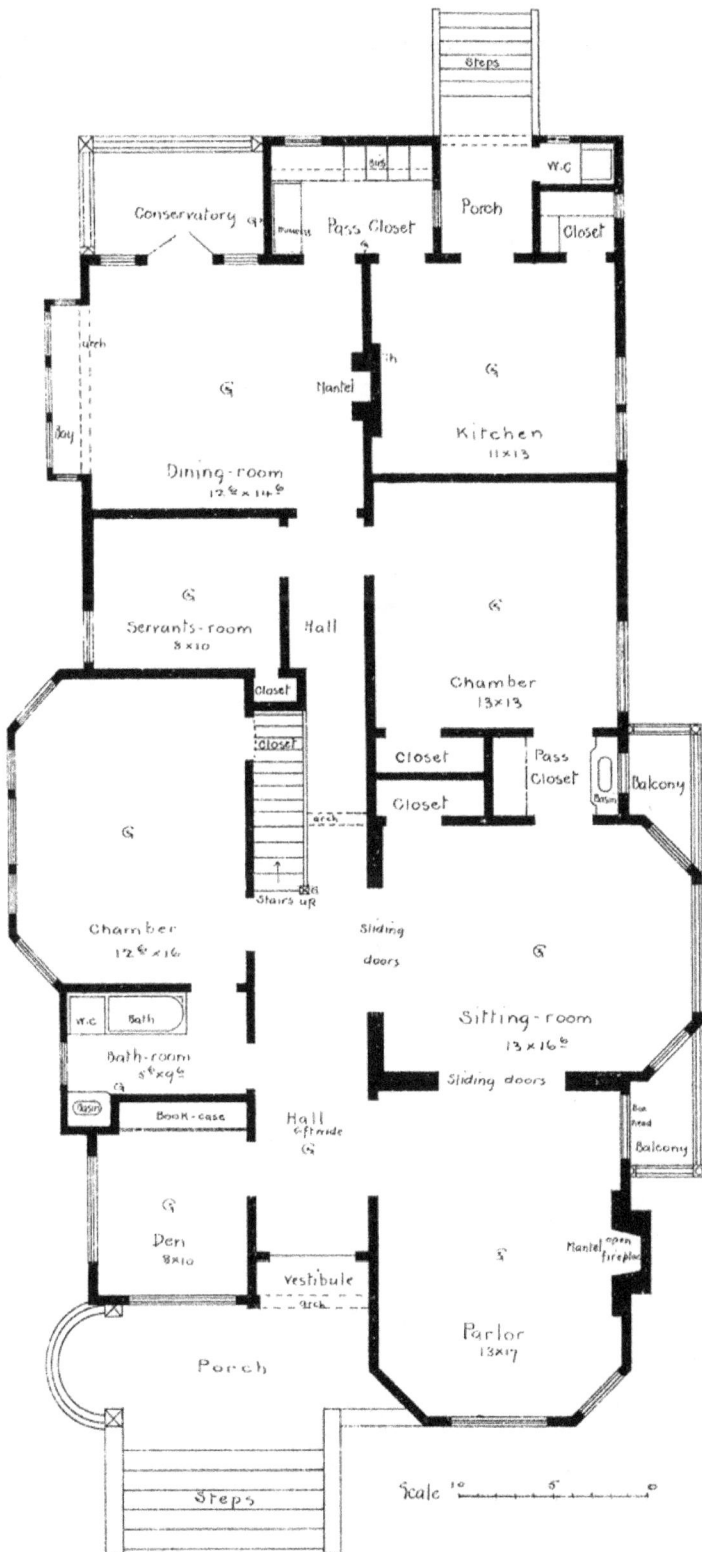

Steps

Conservatory 9ᵗ

Pass Closet

Porch

W.C

Closet

arch

Mantel

G

G

Kitchen
11×13

Dining-room
12⁶×14⁶

Bay

G

G'

Serrants-room
8×10

Hall

Chamber
13×13

Closet

Closet

Closet

Pass
Closet

Balcony

Closet

arch

G

Chamber
12⁶×16

Stairs up

Sliding

doors

G'

W.C Bath

Sitting-room
13×16⁶

Bath-room
8⁶×9⁶

G

Sliding doors

Book-case

Hall
6ft wide

G'

Balcony

G'

Den
8×10

vestibule

arch

Mantel open
fireplace

G'

Parlor
13×17

Porch

Steps

Scale 10   5   0

THE ALAMEDA.

Side Elevation.

Section

Front Elevation

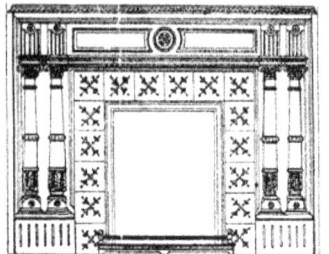

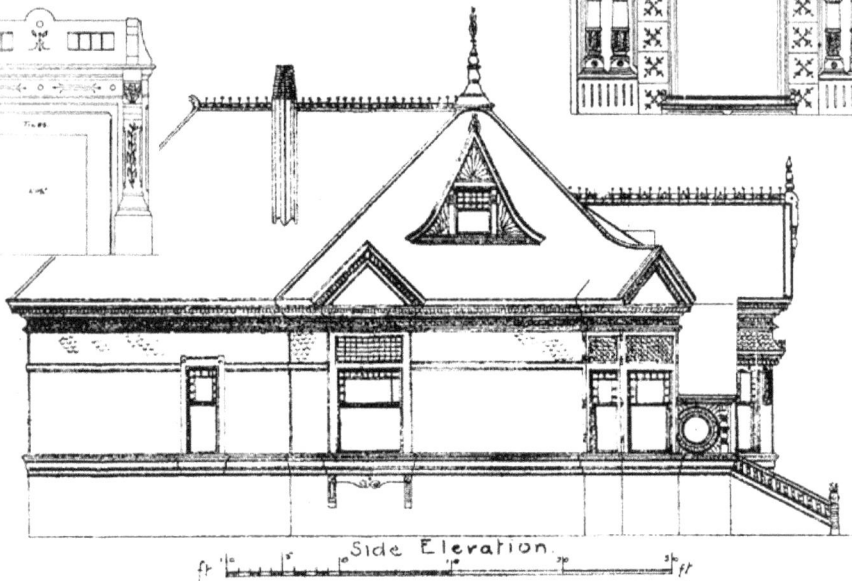

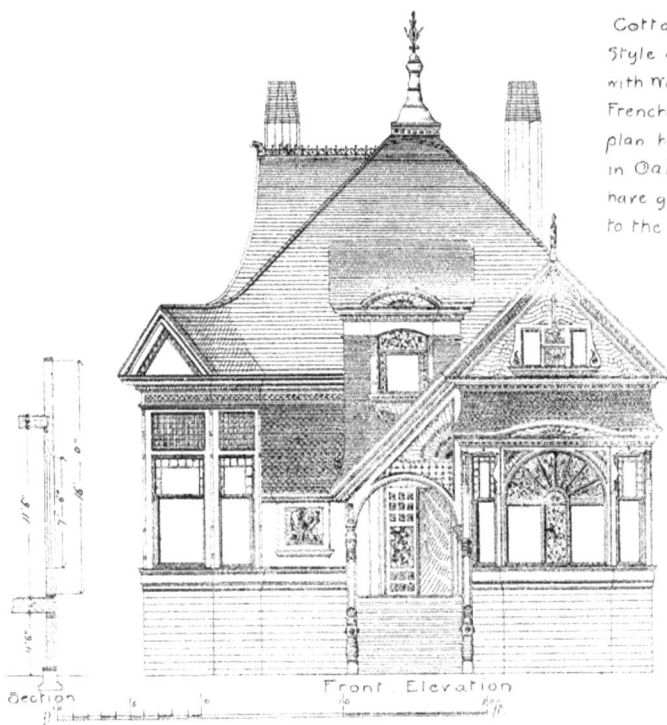

Cottage in the French Renaissance
Style of 7 rooms & Bath. Large Hall
with Wooden Mantel, Tile trimmings
French Arches. Cottages after this
plan have recently been finished
in Oakland & Alameda, and
have given perfect satisfaction
to the Owners.

   The Outside is neat
clean work and would
make an elegant
Cottage dwelling
The Halls & Dining-room
are panel wainscoted in
Lincrusta walton.
The Bath room is in
Red-wood
All the Inside is tinted

Samuel & Jos. Newsom
Architects
504 Kearny St
Top Floor
San Francisco

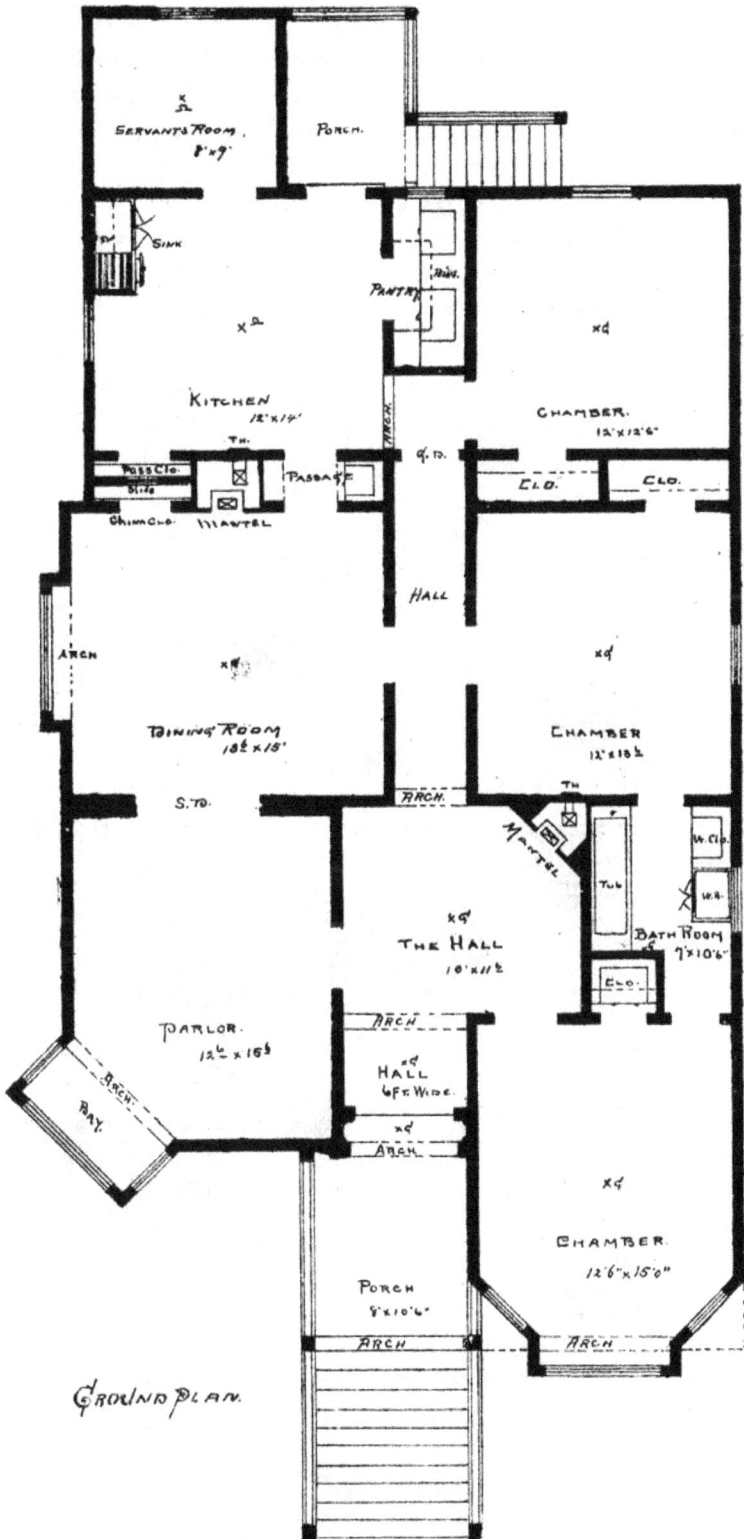

SERVANTS ROOM
8' x 9'

PORCH.

SINK

PANTRY

CHAMBER.
12' x 12'6"

KITCHEN
12' x 14'

CLO.

PASS CLO.
SL. D.

PASSAGE

CLO.

CHIM CLO.

MANTEL

HALL

ARCH

DINING ROOM
18½' x 15'

CHAMBER
12' x 13½'

S. TO.

MANTEL

ARCH.

TUB

W. CLO.

BATH ROOM
7' x 10'6"

THE HALL
10' x 11½'

CLO.

PARLOR.
12' x 15½'

ARCH

ARCH

ARCH

HALL
6 FT. WIDE.

BAY.

ARCH

CHAMBER.
12'6" x 15'0"

PORCH
8' x 10'6"

ARCH

ARCH

GROUND PLAN.

SAUCELITO.

Just the Kind of a Den for the Summer, and Contains 6 large rooms and Den. Would look nell on elevated land. The Exterior is in the Knickerbocker style, and has nide Porch and unique Bay, with Plate Glass Window and Cathedral Glass Transom. Interior finished in Natural manner and stained to imitate Mahogany. Large closets and Pantry. Laundry and Wine Cellar in Basement. Exterior = Painted in Two Shades, Body- Dark Olive. Trimmings Light Olive. Roof-State. and under Water Table-Indian Red

Front Elevation

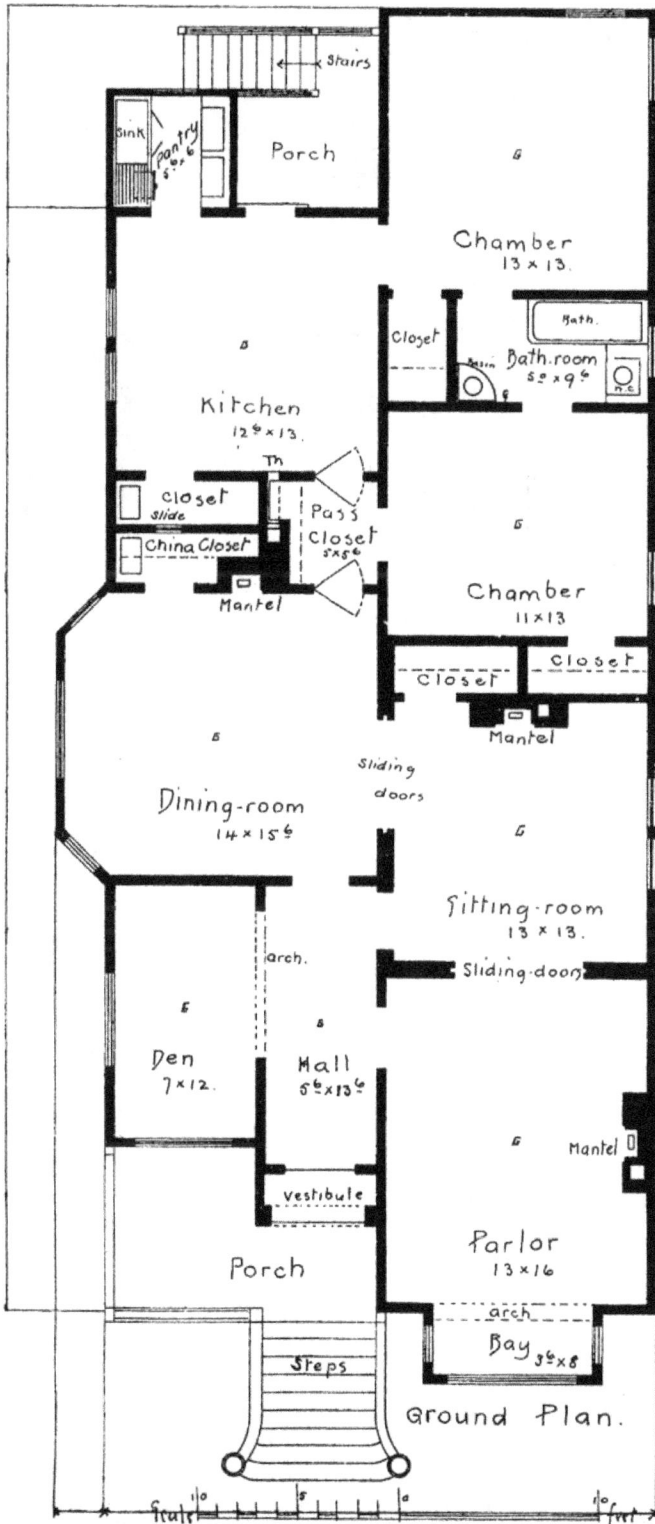

Stairs

Sink Pantry
5⁶x6⁶

Porch

Chamber
13 x 13.

Closet

Bath.

Bath.room
8⁰x9⁶

Basin

w.c.

Kitchen
12⁶x13.

closet
slide

China Closet

Pass
Closet
5x5⁶

Mantel

Chamber
11x13

Closet

Closet

Mantel

Dining-room
14x15⁶

Sliding
doors

Sitting-room
13 x 13.

Sliding-doors

arch.

Den
7x12.

Hall
5⁶x13⁶

Mantel

vestibule

Parlor
13x16

arch

Porch

Bay
3⁶x8

Steps

Ground Plan.

Scale 10   5   0   10 feet

PETALUMA.

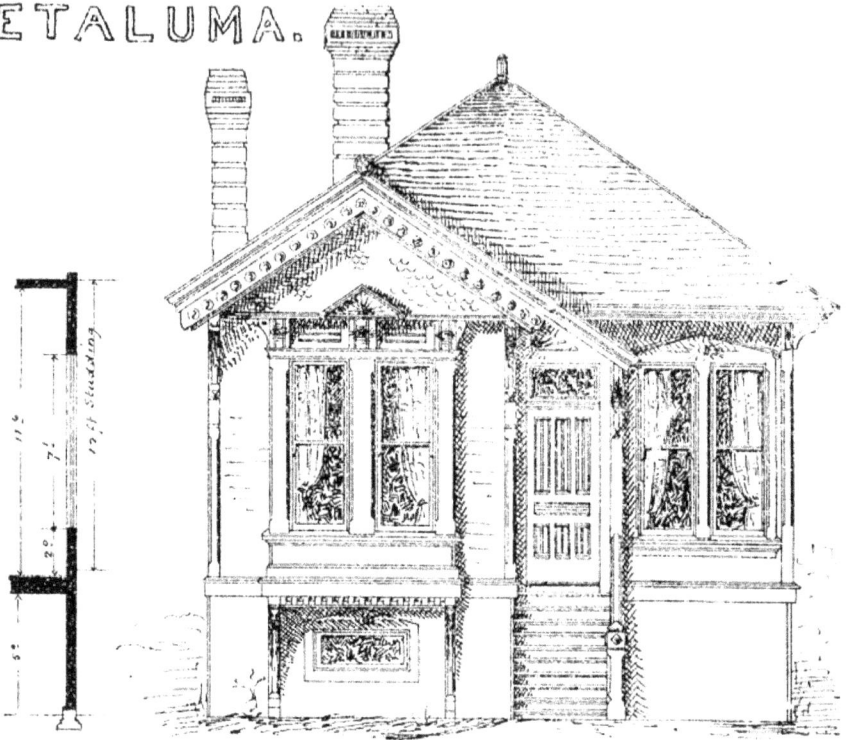

Front Elevation

SAUCELITO.
Cost:

Lumber	$500
Brickwork	140
Sewers	30
Labor	450
Plumbing & Gas Fitting	130
Tinning	40
Millwork	500
Painting	120
Plastering	140
Hardware Nails &c.	90
Mantel	100
Bells	10
Total	$2250

PETALUMA.
Cost

Lumber	$325
Labor	300
Millwork Glass &c	450
Painting	110
Plumbing Gas & Tinning	130
Plastering	125
Mantel	35
Hardware &c.	75
Brickwork & Sewers	110
Total Cost	$1660

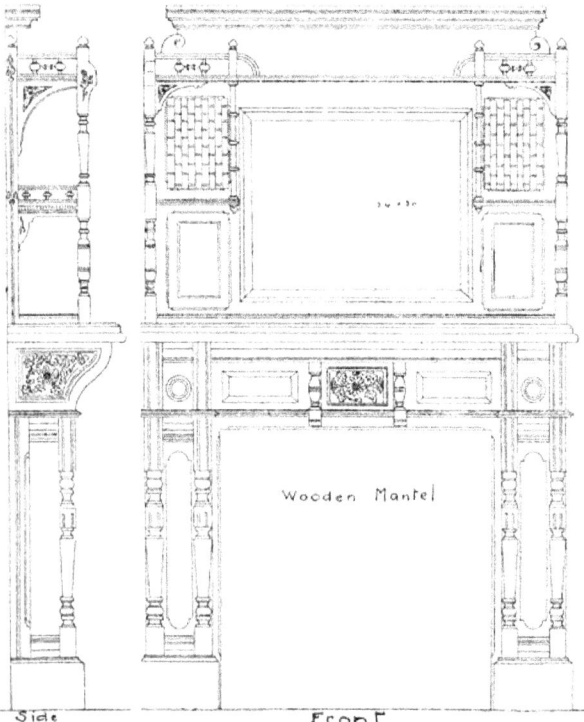

Wooden Mantel

Side   Front

Samuel & NEWSOM,
Jos. C. Architects
504 Kearny St.
:, Top Floor =:
San Francisco
Cal.

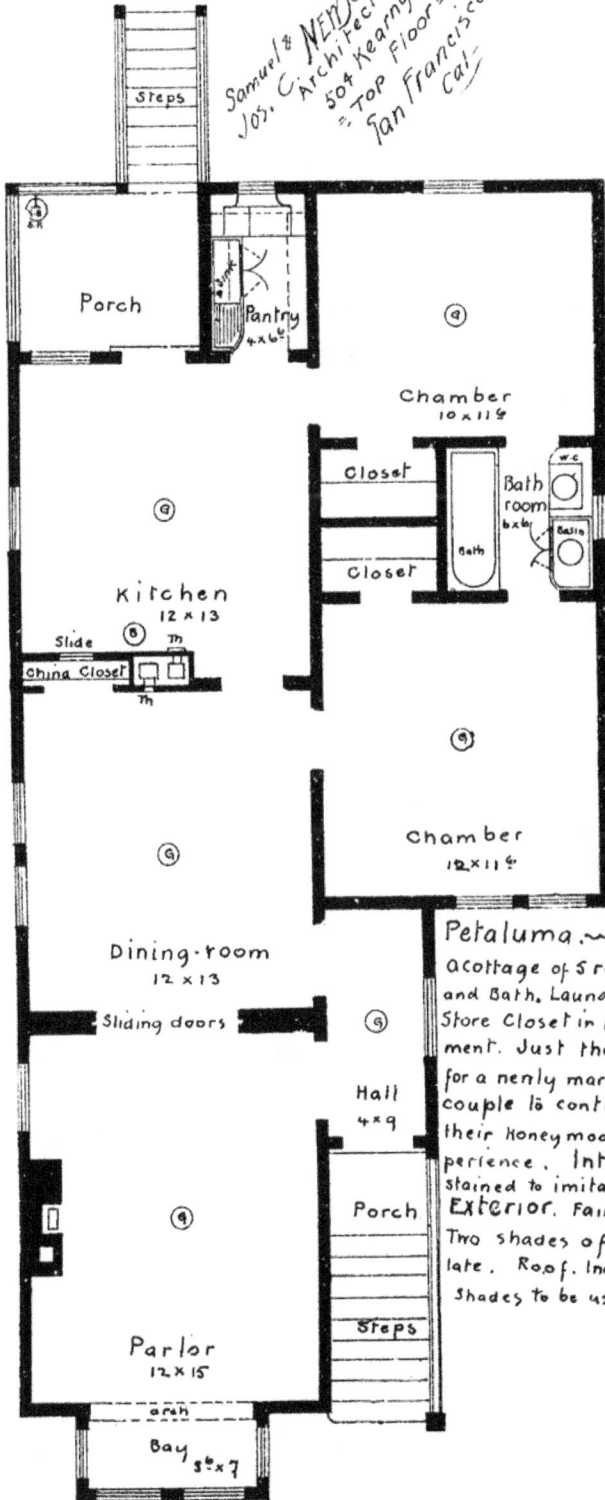

Steps

Porch

Pantry
4 x 6⁶

(a)

Chamber
10 x 11⁴

Closet

Bath room
6 x 6¹

Bath

W.C.

Basin

(g)

Kitchen
12 × 13

Slide

China Closet

(B)

Th

Th

Closet

(g)

Chamber
12 × 11⁴

Petaluma.

A cottage of 5 rooms
and Bath, Laundry &
Store Closet in Base-
ment. Just the Home
for a newly married
couple to continue
their Honeymoon ex-
perience. Interior
stained to imitate Cherry
Exterior. Painted
Two shades of Choco-
late. Roof. Indian Red
shades to be used

Dining-room
12 × 13

Sliding doors

(g)

Hall
4 × 9

Porch

(g)

Steps

Parlor
12 × 15

arch

Bay
3⁶ × 7

GOLDEN GATE PARK.

Two Genteel Cottages one of Five and the other of Six Rooms well laid out, and finished in Polished Red wood, Burl panels, Parlors are good size and arranged for a change in furnishing. The Front Bays of both have Large French Plate Glass windows with Ornamental Stained Glass over, the same also to Front Doors and Transoms over. Open Fireplaces, Wooden Mantels. Electric Bells and Speaking Tubes. They are adapted to families of 3 or 4 persons

Elevation B.   Elevation A.

Estimated Cost
for
Six Rooms A

Lumber $ 450

Millwork (sash)
doors & blinds } 500

Plumbing & Tinning 250

Labor 425

Painting 200

Brick 200

Sewers 75

Hardware 150

Plastering 250

Glass 100

Mantels. 100

Sundries 100

Total Cost $ 2700.

Total Cost
5 Rooms B $ 2500

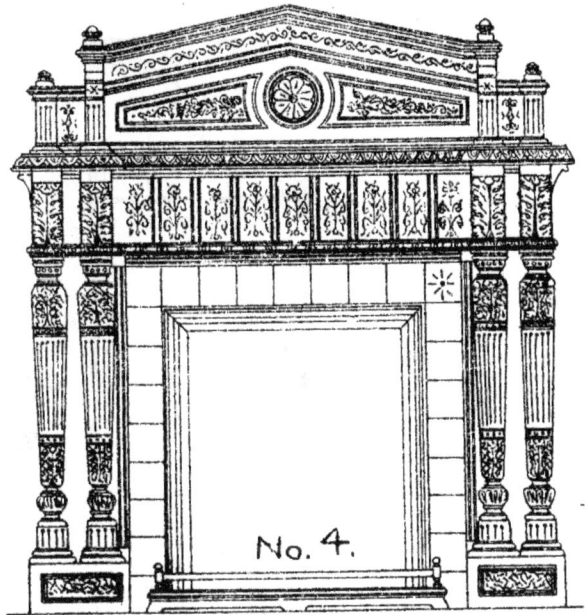

No. 4.

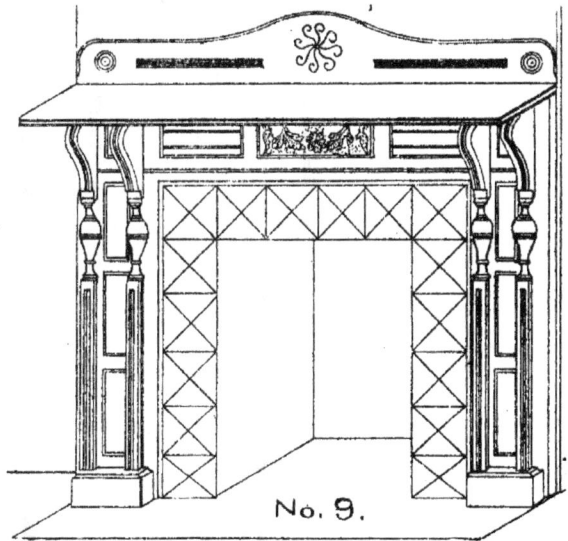

No. 9.

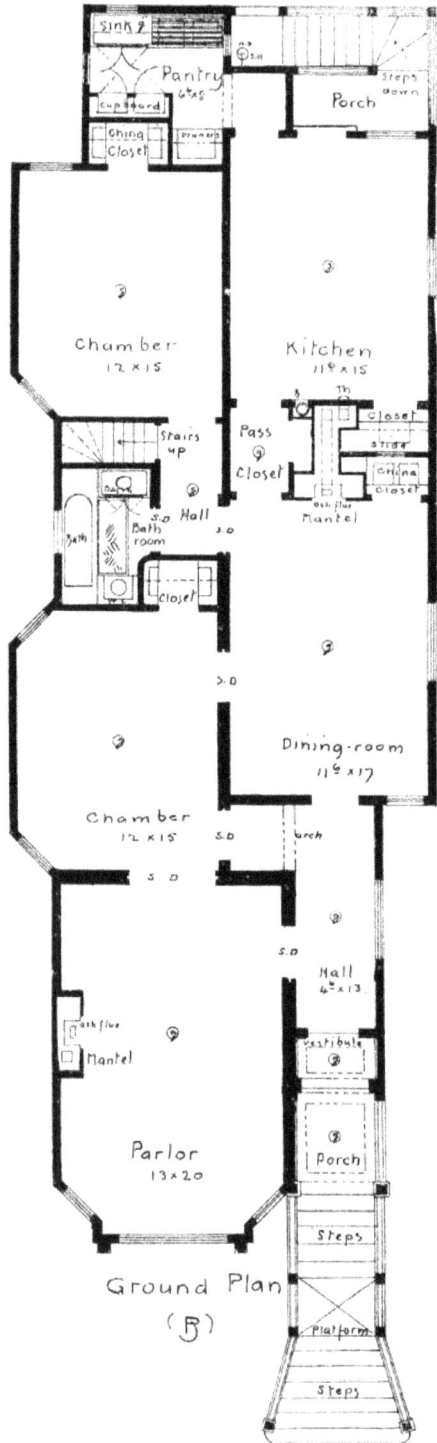

SINK

Pantry
6'×9'

Porch

Steps down

cupboard

China Closet

drawers

Chamber
12×15

Kitchen
11'9"×15

Stairs up

Pass Closet

Closet

altrea

China Closet

S.D Hall

Bath room

Bath

ash flue Mantel

Closet

Dining-room
11'9"×17

Chamber
12×15

S.D

S.D

S.D

S.D

Mantel

ash flue

Hall
4'9"×13

Vestibule

Parlor
13×20

Porch

Ground Plan
(B)

Steps

Platform

Steps

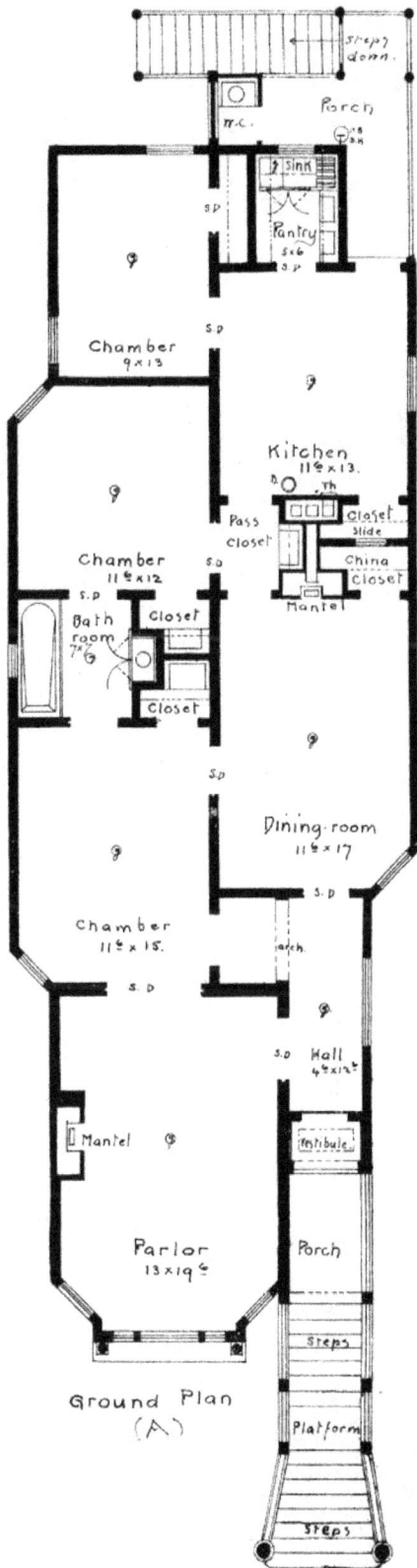

Steps down.

Porch

W.C.

Sink

Pantry
5x6

S.P.

S.P.

Chamber
9x13

S.P.

Kitchen
11½x13.

Pass
Closet

Closet
Slide

China
Closet

Chamber
11½x12

S.P.

Bath
room
7x9

Closet

Closet

Mantel

S.P.

Dining room
11½x17

S.P.

Chamber
11½x15.

arch.

S.P.

Hall
4½x12½

S.P.

Vestibule

Mantel

Parlor
13x19½

Porch

Steps

Ground Plan
(A)

Platform

Steps

PORTLAND.

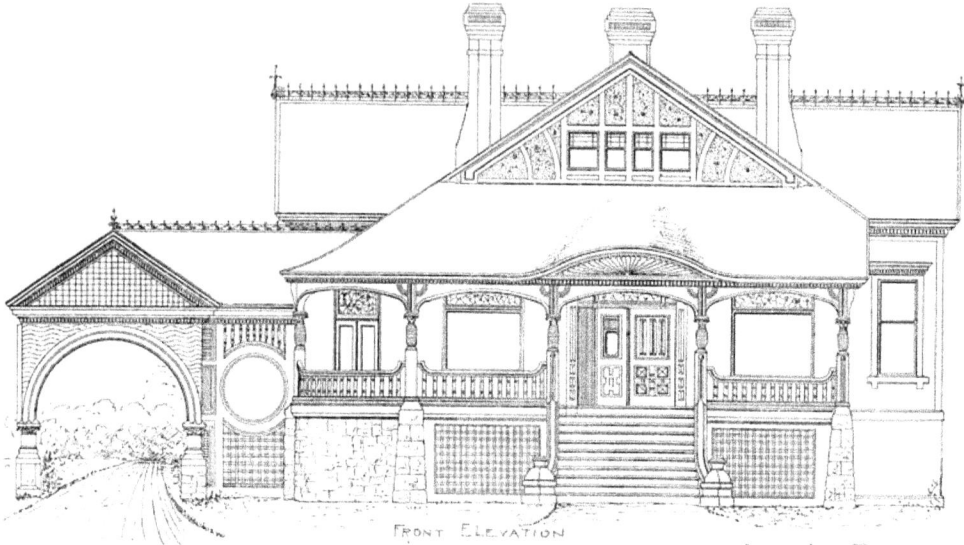

FRONT ELEVATION

Scale = 4ft to the inch
Scale |___|___|___| feet
5   0   10   20

Samuel & Jos. Newsom
ARCHITECTS
no. Kearny St. cor Cal St.
Third Floor
S.F.

An Artistic Cottage with Domed
Reception Hall and Central
Entrance. Foundation is of
Stone. Verandah in Front has
round corner — Reception Hall
is connected with arch to Dining
room — The Fireplaces
are pressed brick
Cost - $5,000.00

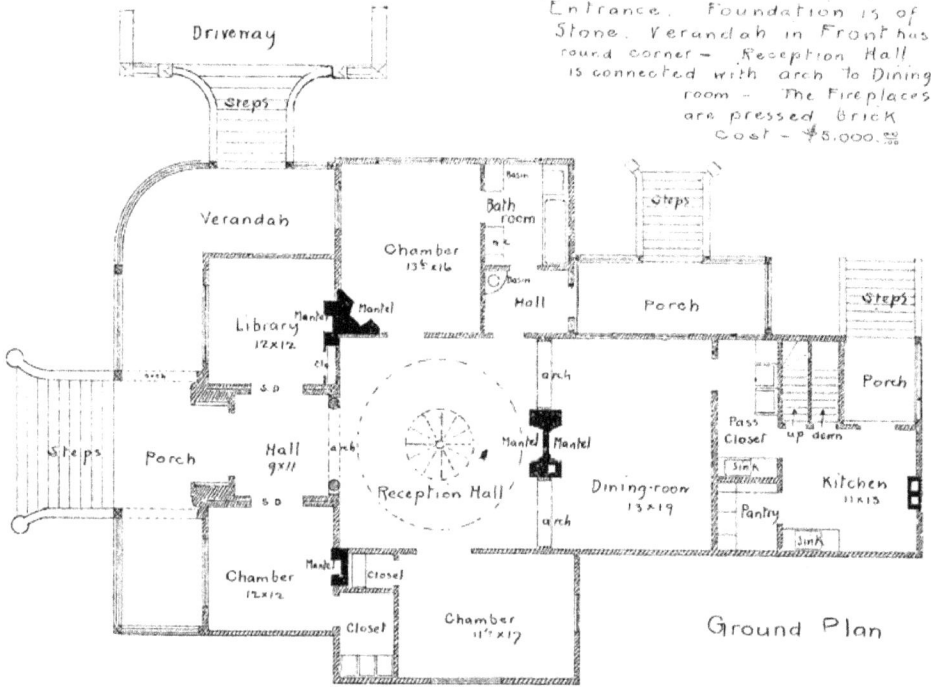

Driveway

Steps

Verandah

Chamber
13 x 16

Bath
room

Basin

Hall

Steps

Porch

Library
12 x 12

Mantel

Mantel

arch

Steps

Porch

Steps

Porch

Hall
9 x 11

arch

Mantel Mantel

Pass
Closet

up down

Reception Hall

Dining-room
13 x 19

Sink

Kitchen
11 x 13

Pantry

arch

Sink

Chamber
12 x 12

Mantel

Closet

Closet

Chamber
11'6 x 17

Ground Plan

Scale |_|_|_|_|_| ft.
10 5   0   10   20   30   40

Sidebaord.

Mantel

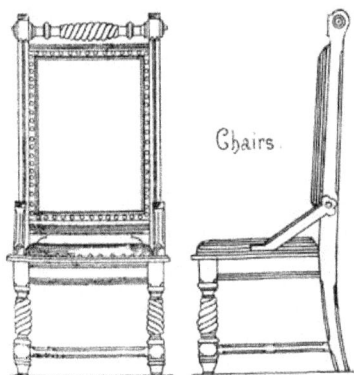

Chairs.

Dining Room Table.

FELTON.

This magnificent appearing Cottage is in the Colonial Style having Gable Porch with Tile filling Turned and carved Posts, and round Balcony on One Side. Steps and Rail curved out to Buttress Posts Parlor Bay has large Circular head Cathedral Glass Transom and large pane of Plate Glass below, and having deep recess with turned Columns on each Side, Gable over finished in fancy Shingles, and carved and turned Verge Board. Chimney tops finished in Pressed Brick Dog toothed panels. Painting Exterior in following colors would give a good contrast. Ground line to Sill Course, Seal Brown, Sill Course to Shingles Shrimp Pink. Shingles- Natural, Main Cornice, Pompeian Red with Raw Sienna Soffit. Roof painted Brown Gray, Sash, Bottle Green. Interior, The Vestibule is finished in natural wood with Tile Floor. Reception Hall off Main Hull has Brick Mantel, and Bay with Moorish windows with Cathedral Glass. Wood arch with Turned Columns and Spindle Filling between Parlors. Pass Closet connect Dining room and Kitchen. Stairs up to attic where rooms could be made if necessary. Stairs to Basement where Laundry. Store room wood & Coal room &c are located. Chambers all good size with ample Closet room

Estimated Cost

Brickwork. Sewers &c	$ 450.00
Labor	900.00
Millwork. Sash, Doors Blinds	1,700.00
Glass and Stairs	250.00
Hardware. Nails &c	125.00
Mantels & Tiles	400.00
Cathedral Glass	100.00
Plastering - Centers	450.00
Plumbing, Tinning & Gas Fitting	350.00
Painting	275.00
Electric Bells & Speaking Tubes	75.00
Lumber	1000.00
Total Cost	$6075.00

FRONT ELEVATION

Ground Plan.

Scale [feet]

Balcony

Reception Hall

Main Hall

Porch

Vestibule

Chamber

Chamber

Chamber

Chamber

Closet

Closet

Closet

Closet

Hall

Hall

Bath room

Tub

Steps

Parlor

Rear Parlor

Dining-room

Mantel

Mantel

Sliding doors

Sliding doors

Pass Closet

China Closet

Kitchen

Porch

Pantry

Sink

Bay.

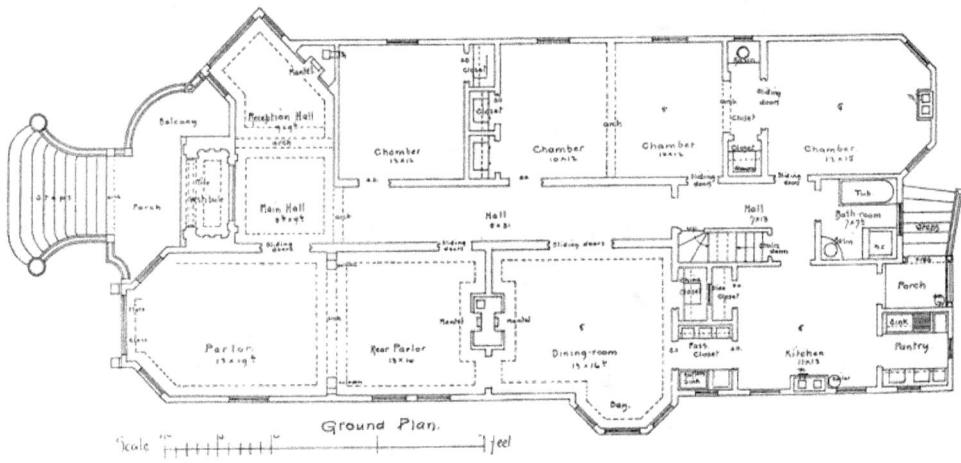

Samuel & Joseph C. NEWSOM
Architects.
504 Kearny St
Top Floor
San Francisco.
Cal.

OAK DALE Nº I

Section   Front Elevation

₁₀ feet.   Nº I

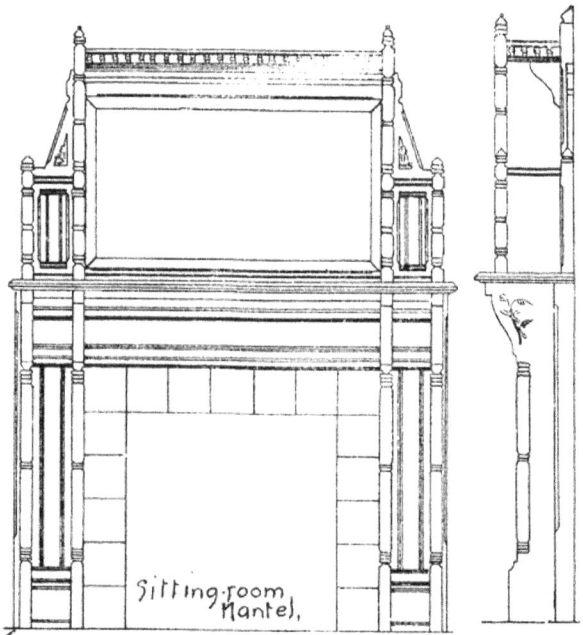

Sitting room Mantel,

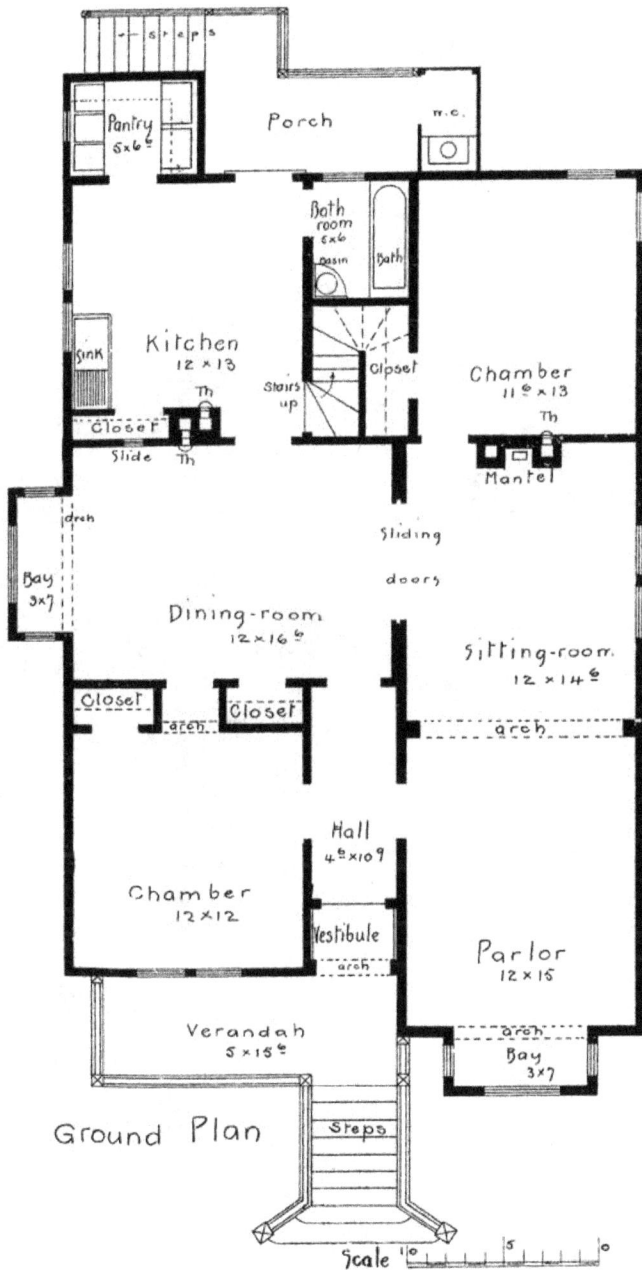

steps

Porch

Pantry
5×6⁶

w.c.

Bath
room
6×6

Bath

basin

Kitchen
12×13

Sink

Chamber
11⁶×13

Th

Closet

Slide

Th

Stairs
up

Closet

Mantel

arch

Bay
3×7

Sliding

doors

Dining-room
12×16⁶

Sitting-room.
12×14⁶

Closet

Closet

arch

arch

Hall
4⁶×10⁹

Chamber
12×12

Vestibule

arch

Parlor
12×15

Verandah
5×15⁶

arch

Bay
3×7

Ground Plan

Steps

Scale

5

10

OAK DALE N°1

~Cost~

Lumber	$450.
Painting	120.
Brickwork & Plastering	270.
Millwork, Glass Sash & Doors	}500.
Plumbing & Tinning	165.
Hardware & Nails &c	90.
Sewers	30.
Mantel	35.
Labor	350.
Total Cost	$2010.

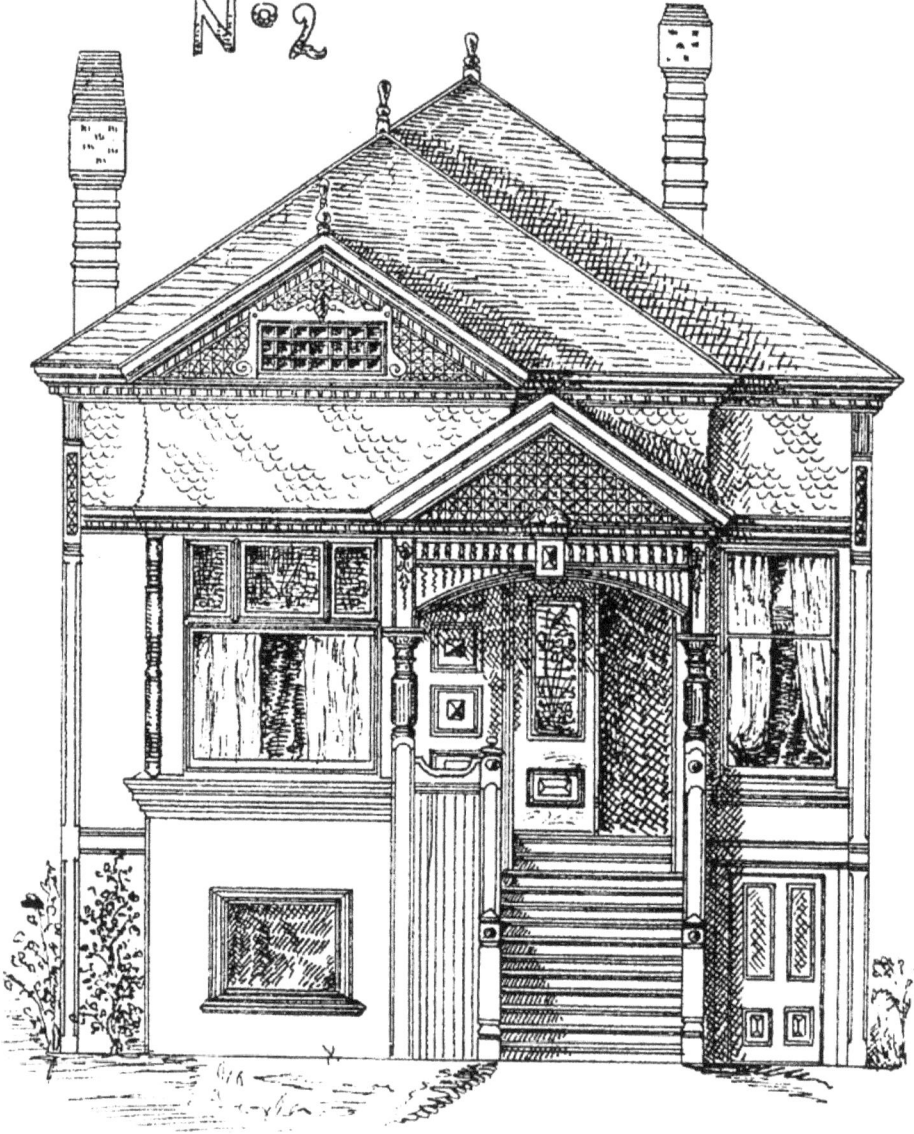

TEMISCAL.

Nº 2

TEMISCAL.
~ Cost ~
N° 2.

Lumber $ 400.
Painting   120.
Brickwork & Plastering 240.
Millwork & Glass   450.
Plumbing & Tinning 160
Hardware & Nails   75
Sewers   30
Labor   300
Bells & Mantel   45
Total Cost $1820

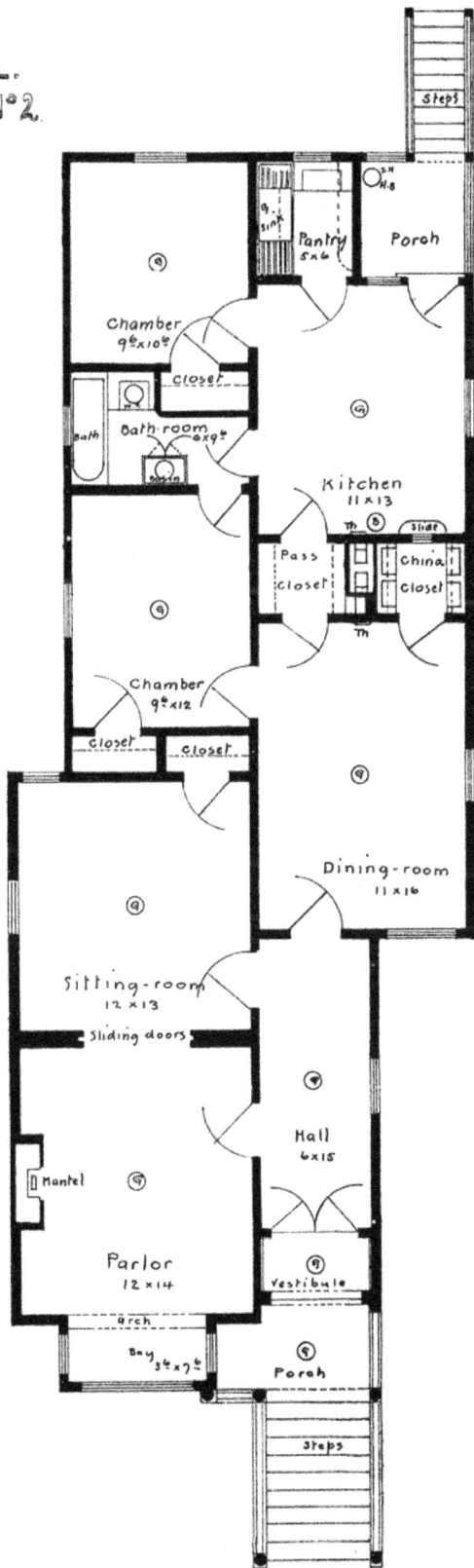

Steps

S.H
W.B

Pantry
5 × 6

Porch

Chamber
9⁰ × 10⁰

Closet

Bath

Bath-room
6 × 9⁴

Kitchen
11 × 13

Slide

Pass
Closet

China
Closet

Chamber
9⁰ × 12

Closet   Closet

Dining-room
11 × 16

Sitting-room
12 × 13

Sliding doors

Hall
6 × 15

Mantel

Parlor
12 × 14

Vestibule

Arch

Bay
3⁴ × 7⁶

Porch

Steps

SANTA ROSA.

No. 1.

Cottage of three
rooms and bath
room

This will make
a neat home for a
small family, or
would do for a Gar-
deners Cottage, or
an artists Studio
with slight changes
it will cost
$750.00

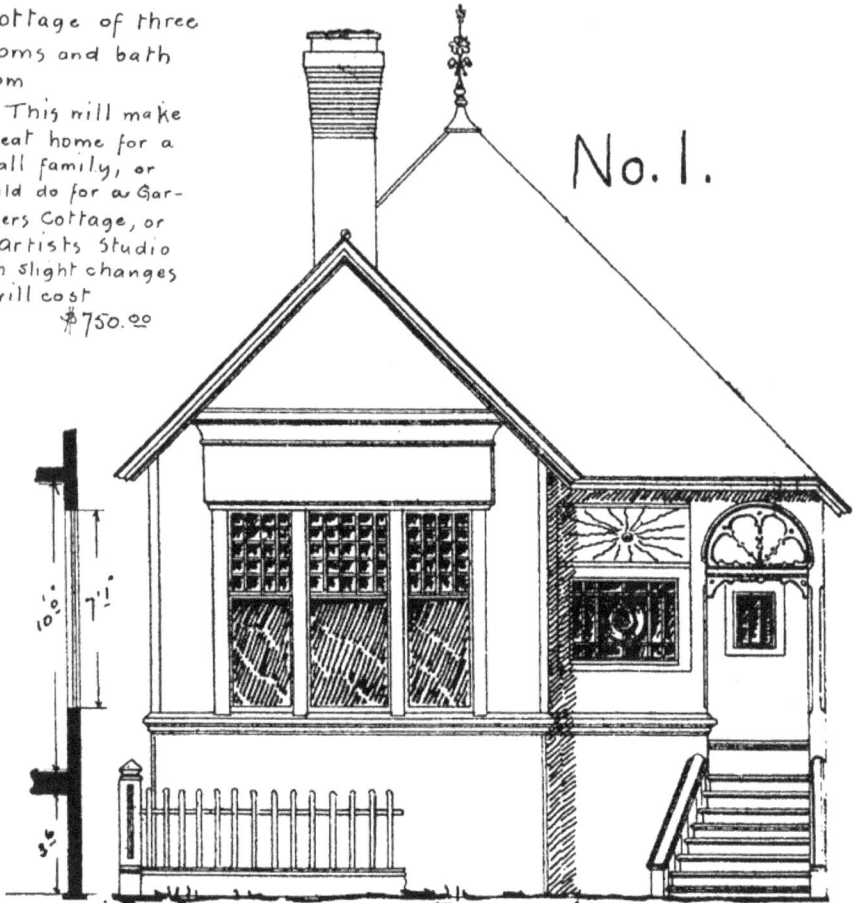

No. 1.

Section.   Front Elevation

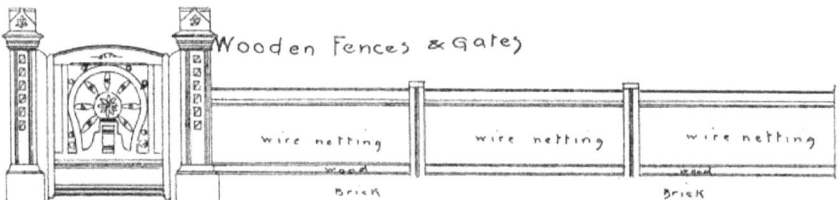

Wooden Fences & Gates

wire netting   wire netting   wire netting

Wood   Wood

Brick   Brick

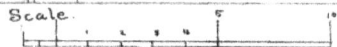

Scale.

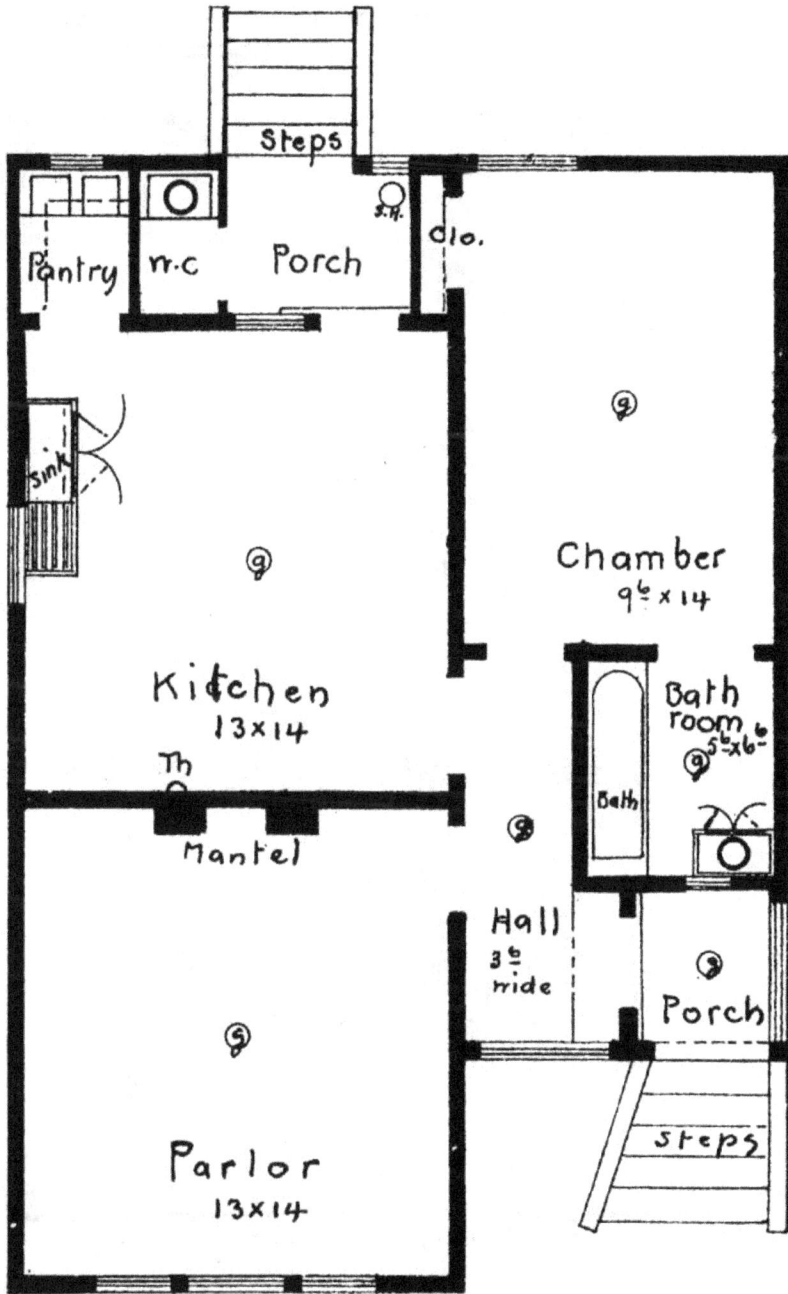

Steps

Pantry | m·c | Porch | s.h. | clo.

sink

g

Chamber
9⁶×14

Kitchen
13×14

g

Bath
room
5⁶×6⁶

Th

Bath

Mantel

g

Hall
3⁶
wide

g

Porch

g

steps

Parlor
13×14

Ground Plan

→No. 2←
a Handy cottage with
6 rooms. a great many
after this plan are
built in Oakland and
Alameda. Cal.
The Front Bay is the
main Feature with the
large Plate Glass light
→Estimated Cost←
Lumber — — — $450
Millwork & Glass — 350
Plumbing & Sewers — 150
Painting — — — — 120
Plastering — — — 140
Hardware — — — — 90
Labor — — — — — 300
Cathedral Glass — — 40
Mantels — — — — 40
Brickwork & chimneys 140
Bells — — — — — 10
Sundries — — — — 40
Total Cost $1870.00

Side Elevation No. 2.

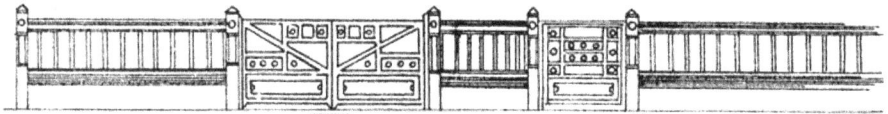

Elevation of Front Fence

Section

Front Elevation No. 2.

Scale

Steps

Porch

2

Chamber
10⁶ × 11⁶

Closet   Closet

closet

Kitchen
11 × 11⁶

Boiler   Th

Closet

Stove

China
Closet

Th

Pass
Closet

2

Chamber
11 × 11⁶

Hall

Bath-room
5⁶ × 8

basin

Closet   basin   Bath

Pantry
4.9 × 6⁶

Sink

Dining-room
11⁶ × 14

2

Chamber
11 × 11⁶

8. D

Hall
5 × 11⁶

Vestibule

Porch

Steps

Parlor
11⁶ × 12

Mantel

arch

Bay
4 × 8

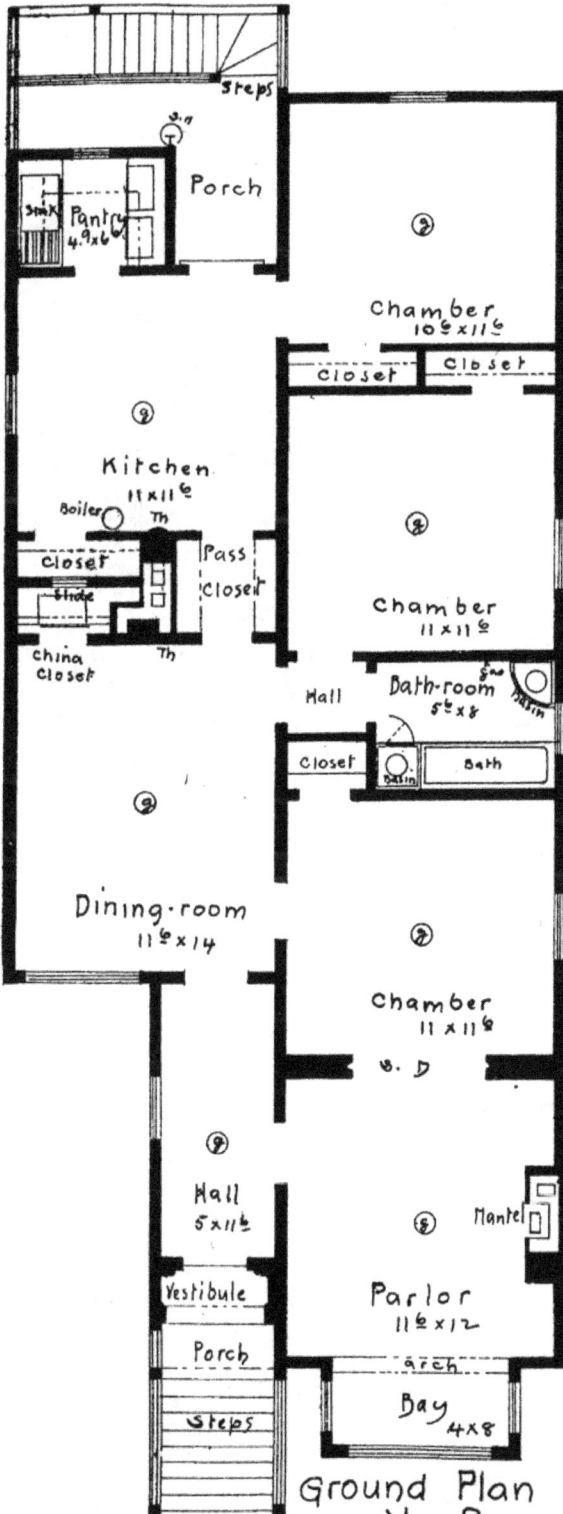

Ground Plan
No. 2.

TIBURON.

Estimated Cost:

Brickwork Centers &c.	$200.00
Labor	400.00
Millwork and Hardware Cases	730.00
Hardware Nails &c.	80.00
Mantels	100.00
Cathedral Glass	75.00
Plastering Center	175.00
Plumbing Piping & Gas Fitting	200.00
Painting	170.00
Bells	30.00
Lumber	560.00
Total Cost	$2,130.00

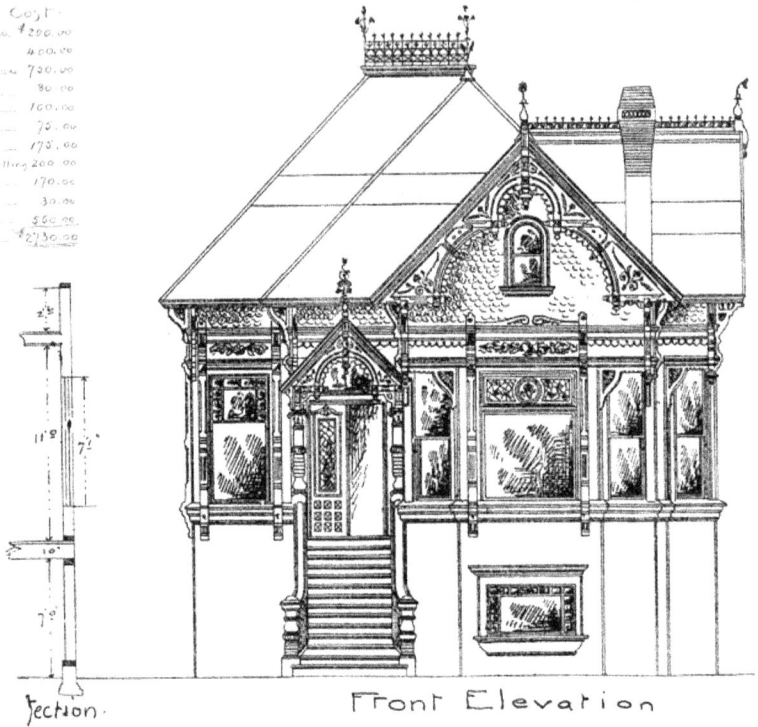

Section.   Front Elevation

Scale   5   0   10   20 Feet

A Handsome Cottage in the Modern Swiss Style or Picturesque, having Gable Porch with neat filling and turned Columns and curved cap. Steps and Rail curved out to Buttress Posts, which make a very imposing approach Front and Side Gables the same, with large Cathedral Glass Transome Window in Parlor making a marked feature in the Building. The Interior is arranged to economize space as much as possible, the Hall entering to the Parlor and Dining-room, each having Marbleized Iron Mantels, and Octagon Ends forming Bays— off Dining room is Chamber and Pass Closet to Kitchen. Bathroom is placed between the two Chambers. Off Kitchen is Stairs to Attic. Pantry with Sink in Same, and Laundry which acts as Pass Closet to Rear Porch, said Porch being enclosed Two Chambers in Attic. Basement unfinished except hood and coal room— This makes a very convenient and desirable house to build

Diningroom Interior.

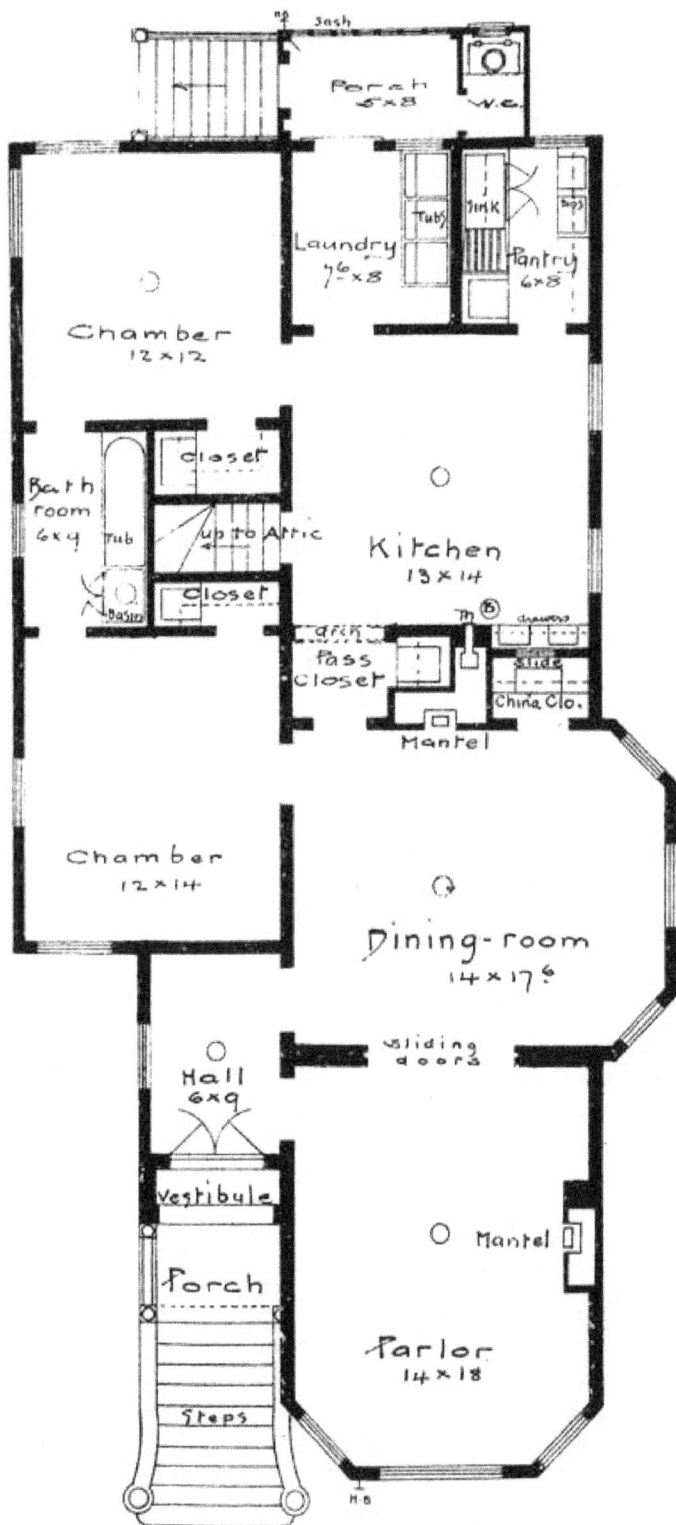

Sash

Porch
5×8

W.c.

Tub Sink

Laundry
7'6×8

Pantry
6×8

Chamber
12×12

Closet

Bath room
6×9

Tub

up to Attic

Closet

Kitchen
13×14

Basin

dark Pass Closet

Th drawers

Slide

China Clo.

Mantel

Chamber
12×14

Dining-room
14×17.6

Sliding doors

Hall
6×9

Vestibule

Mantel

Porch

Parlor
14×18

Steps

M.B.

Ground Plan.

SUNNYSIDE

House of 8 rooms
and Bath. Parlors
double with Decorated
arch. Mantel of Wood
Ebonized and Art
Tiles.

The Dining-room &
Kitchen & Large
Pantries, Wash Tubs &
Hood & Coal in
Basement.

Servants rooms in attic looking
out in Rear.   Doors & Transoms
all in Art Glass :
Hall Window the same
Sitting room has large
Plate Glass Window
Dining-room the same
Antique Glass Margins
Chimney on outside
laid up in Black mortar
and Art Tiles.

Side Elevation

Front Elevation

		Cathedral glass.	$	150
Lumber	$ 580 00	Hardware, nails &c	$ 150	00
Painting	150 00	Mantels	100	00
Brickwork	200 00	Labor	505	00
Millwork.	600 00	Bells & Tubes	45	00
Plastering	250 00	Fences	120	00
Plumbing	250 00	Cement walks	100	00
Sewers	100 00	Total Cost.	$ 3300	00

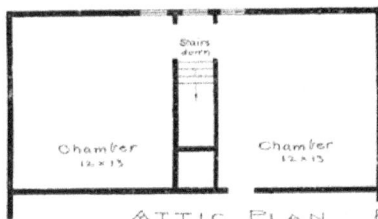

Detail of Front Gable.

Rear View.

In. 1' 6" 8' 9' 10"   1   2   3   4   5 Ft.

ATTIC PLAN

Chamber
12 × 13

Stairs down

Chamber
12 × 13

House of 8 rooms
and Bath. Parlors
double with Decorated
arch. Mantel of Wood
Ebonized and Art
Tiles.
The Dining-room &
Kitchen & Large
Pantries, Wash Tubs &
Wood & Coal in
Basement.

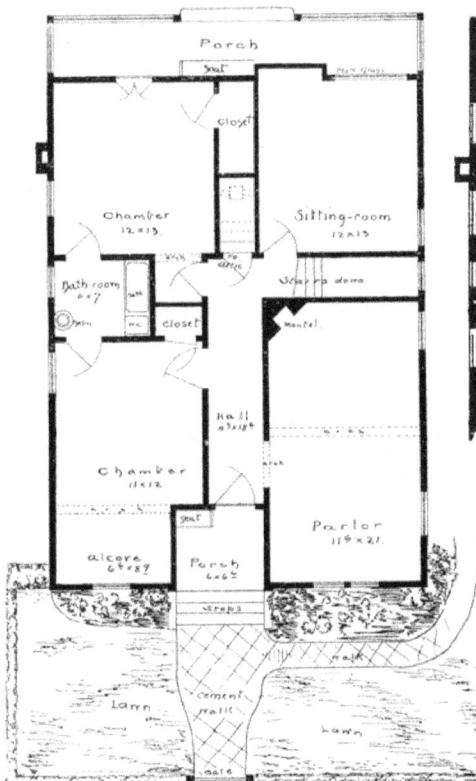

FIRST FLOOR PLAN

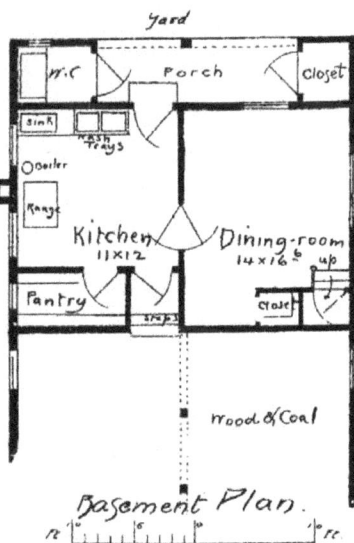

Porch

Seat

Plate Glass

Closet

Chamber
12 × 13

Sitting-room
12 × 13

Bath room
6 × 7

w.c

Stairs down

closet

Mantel

Chamber
11 × 12

Hall 11 × 18 ft.

arch

alcove
6' × 8' 2"

Seat

Porch
6 × 6 ½

Steps

Parlor
11 2" × 21

Lawn

cement walk

walk

Lawn

Gate

Fr.   10   15 Ft.

Basement Plan.

Yard

W.C

Porch

Closet

Sink

Wash Trays

Boiler

Range

Kitchen
11 × 12

Dining-room
14 × 16 ½

up

Pantry

Steps

Closet

Wood & Coal

Ft.   5   10   15 Ft.

Driveway

FERNDALE.

A Picturesque Dwelling of 10 rooms and 2 servants rooms in Attic. Exterior effects are the different styles of embellishments Rough Plaster, Shingle, Pressed Brick and Terra Cotta. The Entrance and surroundings to be of Brick and Arched and Ornamented. The Cornice to be of Plaster and carved Ornamental work. The Octagon Bay on Lower Floor is carried up and a circular Bay is formed, which is surmounted with a Slate covered Tower tapering to a carved and Turned Ornament with a wrought Iron Finial Bronzed. The Interior. The Hall with its highly finished Stair and Mantel is entered from the Entrance Hall off which is the Den, opposite which is the Drawing-room with Octagon Bay and connected with Sitting-room by Spindle Arch, off Sitting-room is an Alcove with Shelves for Flowers. Connected by Sliding doors with Sitting-room is the Dining-room, corner Mantel & Balcony. The Rear Stair connect half way up with Main Stairs, and both continue up the one Stair, thereby saving the space otherwise occupied by Rear Stairs (an odd feature) The Kitchen is large and well ventilated, has Range, Large Closets and Pantry.

On the upper floor are 5 chambers, all having the necessary large Closets and Modern conveniences. Two Servants rooms in Attic Laundry &c in Basement.

Sketch Elevation

Scale

Samuel & Jos. C. Newsom
Architects
504 Kearny St.
cor. California St.
San Francisco
Ca.

≈Top Floor.≈

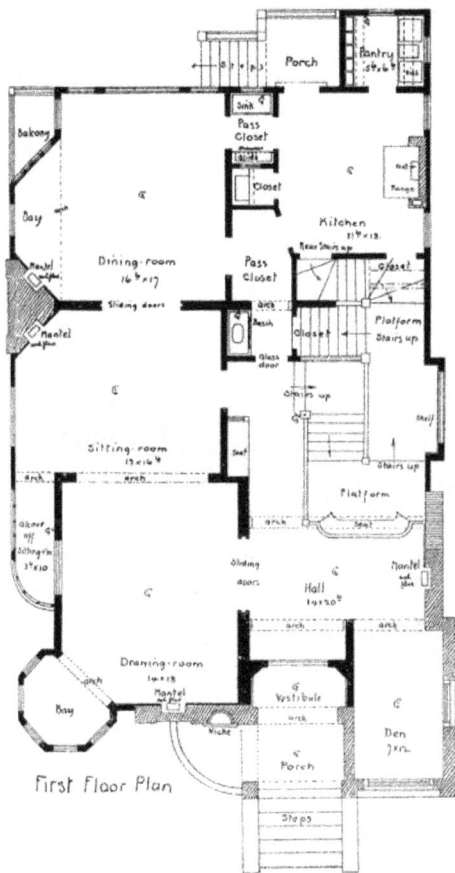

First Floor Plan

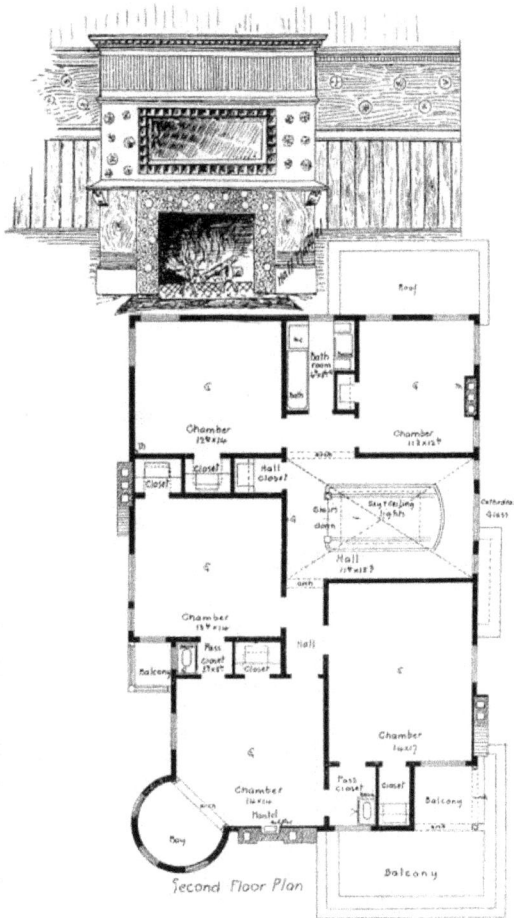

Second Floor Plan

Estimated Cost

Lumber	$1.000.00
Millwork	1.100.00
Plastering	500.00
Painting	300.00
Plumbing & Gas Fitting	350.00
Tinning	60.00
Labor	1.000.00
Bells & Tubing	50.00
Brickwork & Sewers	350.00
Hardware Nails &c	200.00
Cathedral Glass	150.00
Iron work	20.00
Mantels	250.00
Slate Roofing & Sundries	150.00
Total	$5460.00

PIEDMONT.

This design   in which are suspended   meet the ceilings are the   This would make
is for a 12 room residence in the Free   the curtains.   same, the center ornaments   a suitable home
or Knickerbocker Style. The outside   The halls are tinted   are gilded and colored   for a family of
walls are covered with Redwood Shingles   in subdued olive and grey   to match the rooms.   good taste.
varnished and left in the natural color.   tinted with deep friezes.   The Dining room is
The interior is finished in California   in light Blues, and Old   colored Pompeian Red   Samuel Newsom
Redwood. Arches in Parlor and Dining   Gold with Gold lines at   with friezes &c same as   Architects
room are made of Cherry Spindle work   points, their colors   balance of house.   509 Kearny St
                                                                                        4th Floor
                                                                                        San Francisco. Cal.

Front Elevation

Scale   10   5   0   10   20 feet

Side Elevation

Scale 10 5 0 10 20 feet

Estimated Cost		
Excavation. Brickwork & Drains —————	$500	00
Lumber —————————	1550	00
Millwork. Sash, Doors Blinds & Glass ————	1300	00
Labor ———————	1300	00
Mantels —————	300	00
Cathedral Glass ————	300	00
Bells & Hardware ———	300	00
Plumbing & Tinning ———	500	00
Plastering Centers &c. ———	550	00
Painting ————	425	00
Sundries ————	300	00
Total Cost ———	$7125	00

Veranda.

Stairs up.   Hall

Pantry
5⁶×6

Serrants
room
9⁶×9⁶

slide

Closet

china Closet

Bay
sash

Kitchen.
12⁶×13.

Pass. Closet
6×7

Shelf

Hall

w.c

arch

Stairs
up

Dining-room
13×14⁶

Mantel

Book
Case

arch.

Mantel.

Sitting-room
13⁶×14⁶

arch

Hall
10×25⁴

Parlor
14×26

Veranda

Bay

Steps.

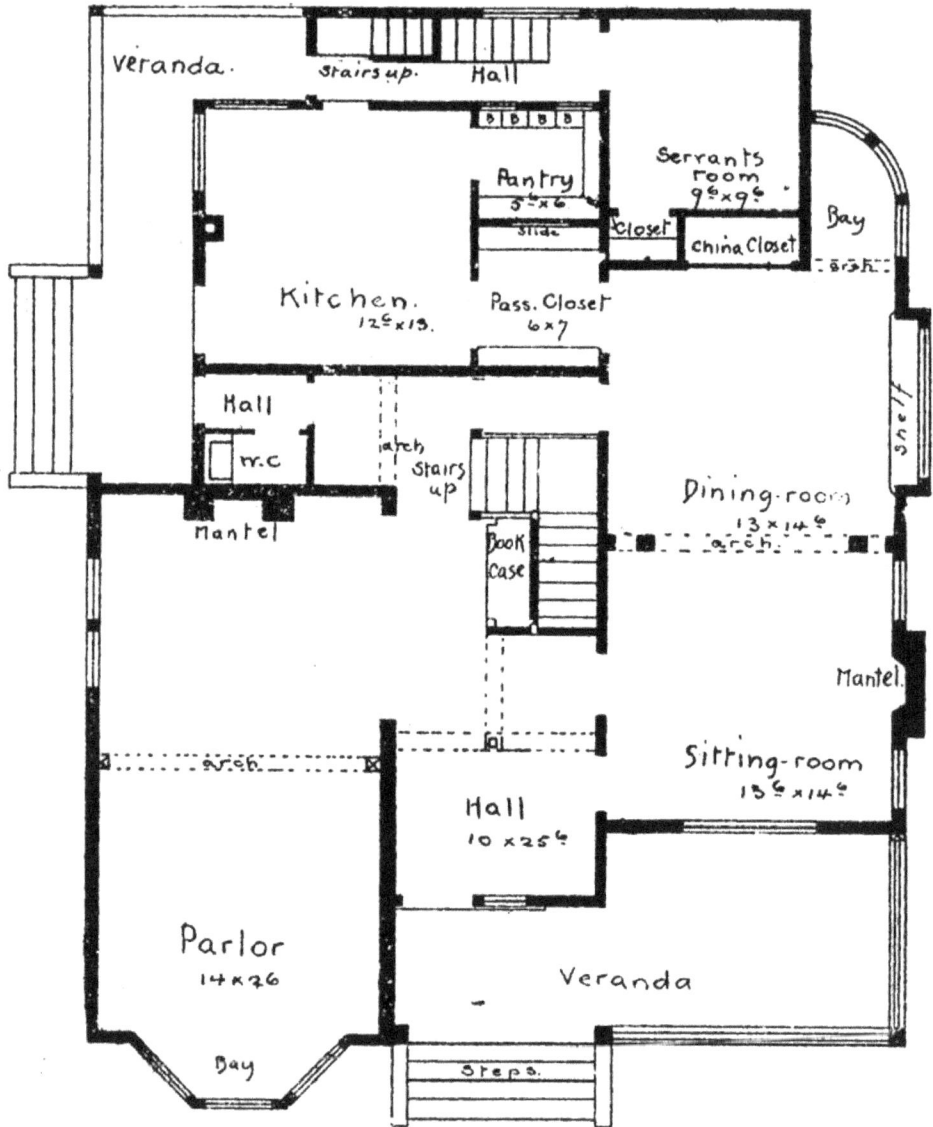

First Floor Plan

Scale   1⁰   5   0   1⁰   2⁰ feet

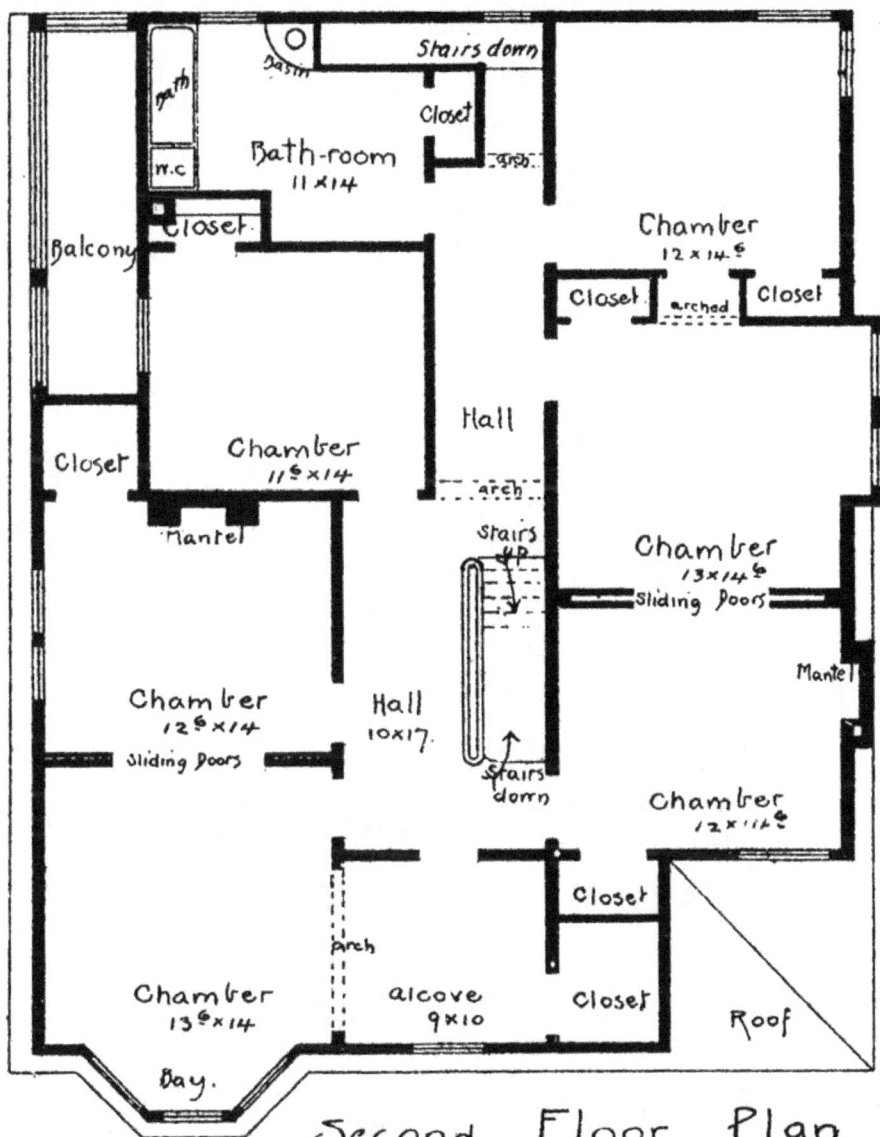

Second Floor Plan

SAN LORENZO

Ten rooms and Bath, Rear part of Basement finished containing Wine Cellar, Store room and Laundry. First Floor has Double Parlors, Large Hall, with Platform Stairs. Dining-room and large size Kitchen with Servants room Pass Closet and Pantry thereoff. Second Story has 4 large Bed-rooms and one Childs or Nurse-room, there is a Dumb Waiter and Clothes Chute in convenient place. Basins are placed where most necessary. The Exterior has large and airy Verandah, Square Bays, tastely filled Gables, all surmounted

Front Elevation

Scale for Plans feet

Sink

Th

Pantry

Serrants-room
10 x 10⁶

Pass
Closet

Kitchen
13⁶ x 15

Porch

Steps

Clo

Dumb
waiter

Stairs up

Hall

China
closet

Closet

Mantel Mantel

arch

Bay

Dining room
13⁶ x 16

Sitting-room
13⁶ x 16⁶

S. D

Basin
Lavatory

Mantel

Stairs
up

Parlor
13 x 19

Verandah

Hall

9⁶ wide

arch

Closet Vestibule

Bay

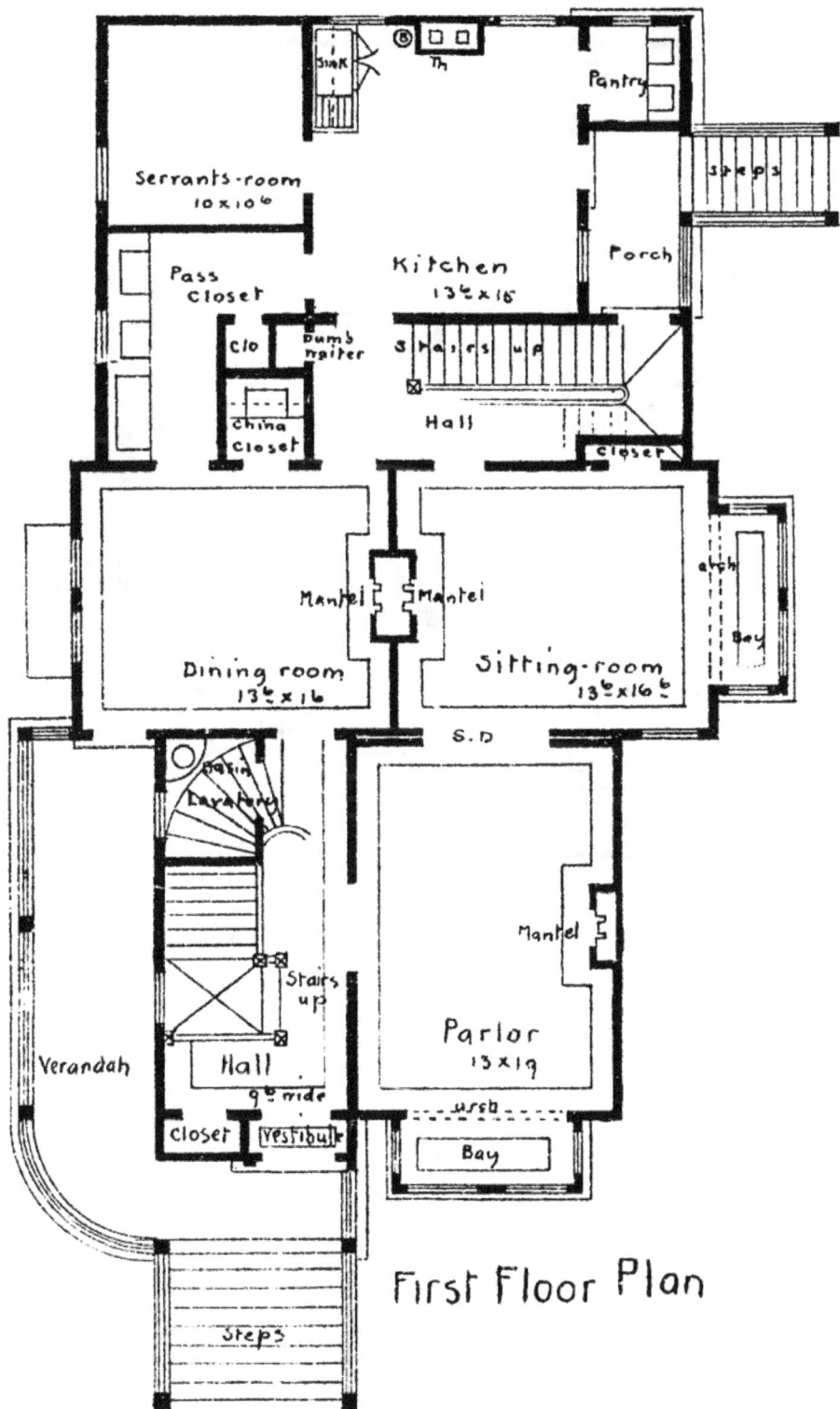

First Floor Plan

Steps

Basin Basin
Th

Childs room
8 x 8⁶

Closet

Chamber
12⁵ x 14⁵

Balcony

Bath
Dumb waiter
Closet
Stairs up

Bath room
7 x ⁶
Stairs down

Closet

Chamber
12 x 13⁶

Hall
3⁶

Th

Chamber
13⁵ x 15

Balcony

niche
Niche
Stairs down

Closet
Basin
Basin
Closet

Closet
arch

Mantel

alcove
9 x 10⁵

Chamber
13 x 16

Balcony

Balcony

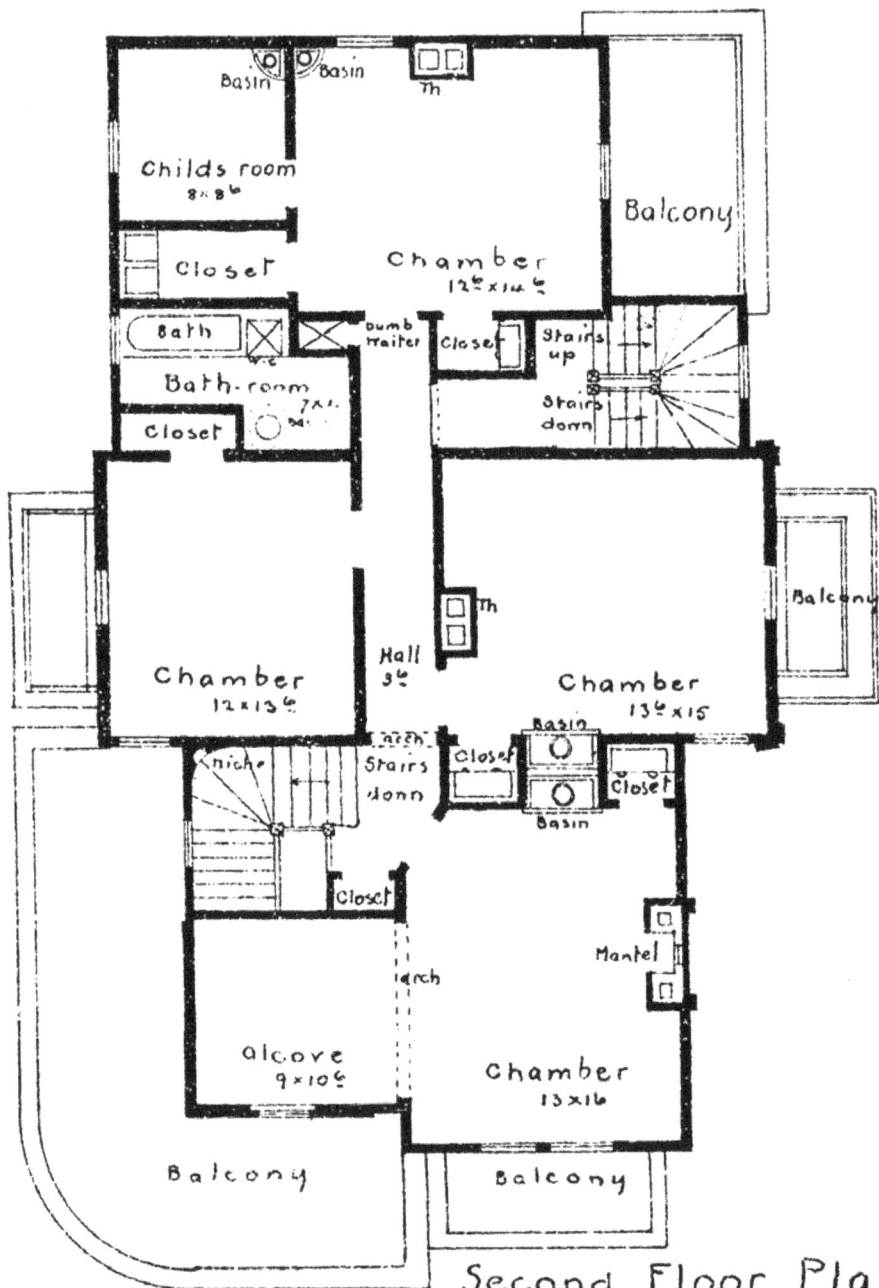

Second Floor Plan

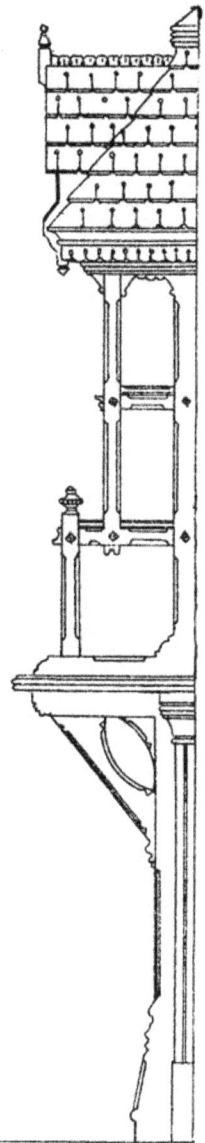

Samuel & Jos. C. Newsom
Architects
504 Kearny St.
Top. Floor
S. F.

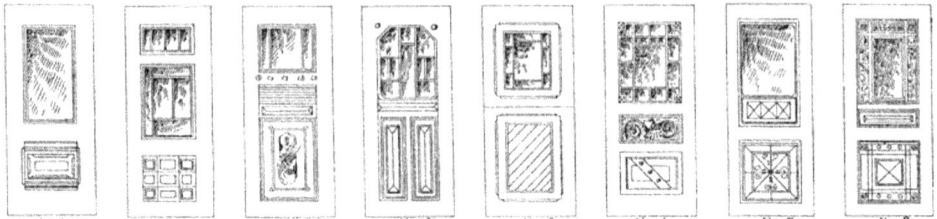

No 1.   No 2.   No. 3.   No. 4.   No. 5   No. 6   No. 7   No. 8.

by Square Tower   Estimated Cost.   Brick work & Sewers 280,00   Iron work
The Style is   Millwork &c. $1200,00   Mantels   200.00   Total Cost   35 00
Eastlake.   Lumber   1100,00   Hardware, Nails &c 150 00 $5540.00
    Labor   1000,00   Cathedral Glass   100.00
    Plumbing, Tinning }   Bells & Tubing   50.00
    & Gas Fitting   450.   Scale for plans
    Painting   325
    Plastering   450

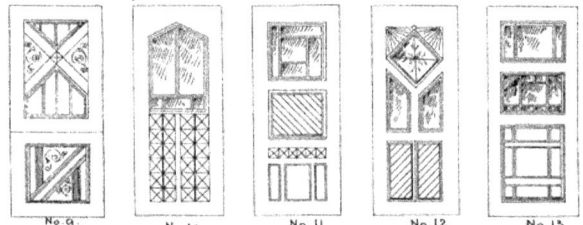

No. 9   No. 10   No. 11   No. 12   No. 13

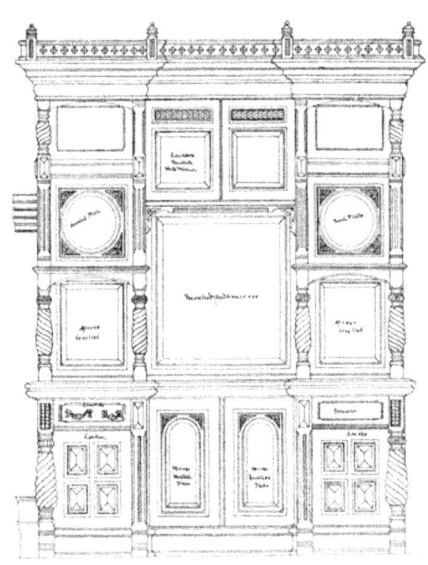

Side board

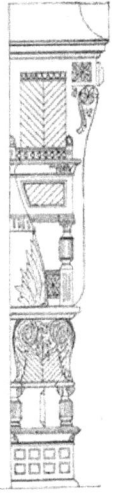

Wooden
Mantels

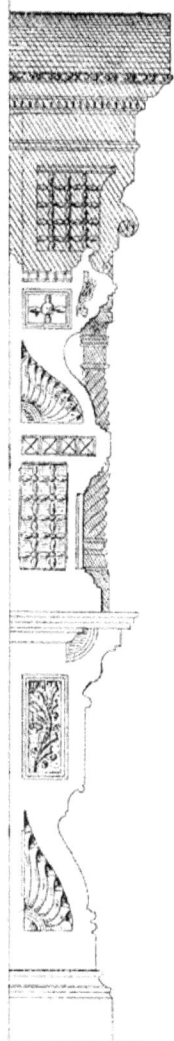

Drawn by Samuel C. Newsom

Architects

504 Kearny St

S.F.

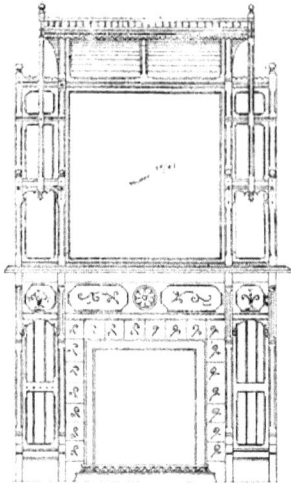

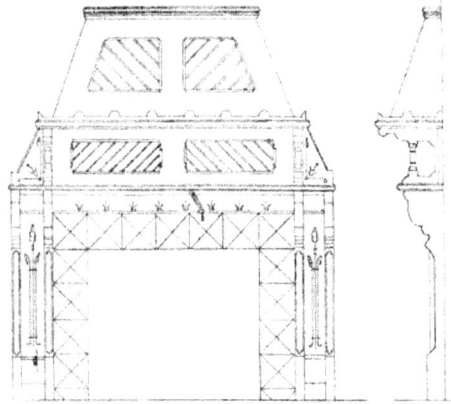

Wooden Mantels

Samuel & J. C. Newsom, Architect
504 Kearny St.
Top Floor
San Francisco.
Cal.

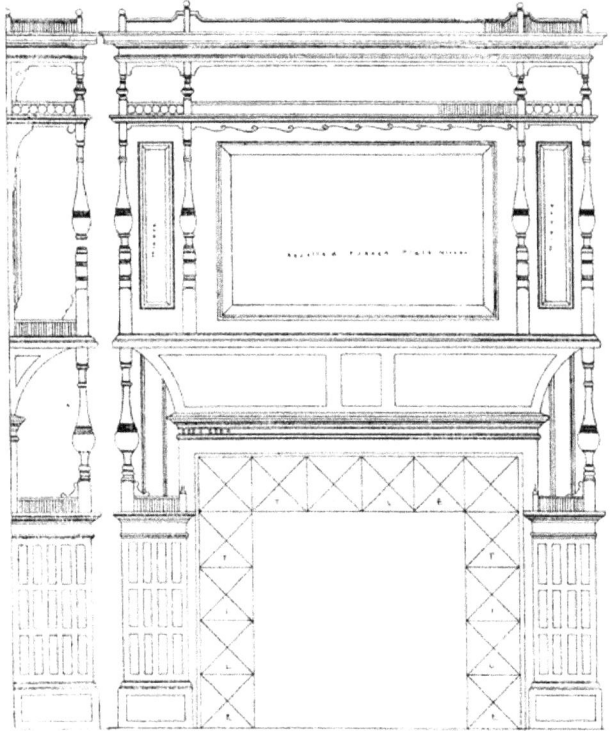

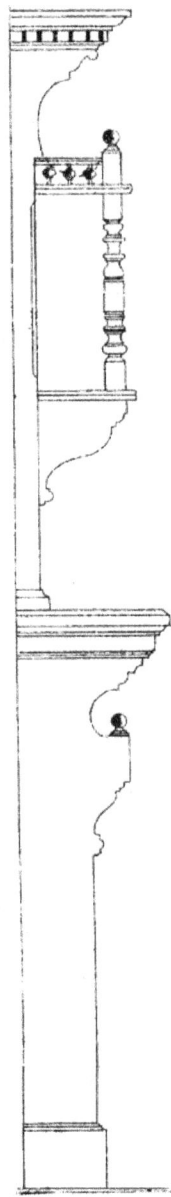

LAKE CHABOT.

A Suburban Dwelling, 8 rooms and Bath. Exterior finish as shown. Interior Painted and Grained Mahogany Shades to Windows. Spanish Cedar Staircase, enclosed in Spindle work. Sand finished walls, tinted. Large Closets Wooden Mantels, Ornamented with Bronze Ornaments. Tiled Hearths and facings. Tiles back of Bath Tub, Basins and Sinks. Hardwood floors to Dining-room and Main Hall. Sliding doors hung above. Bronze Hardware. Best of Plumbing. Cherry Picture Moulding.

Front Elevation

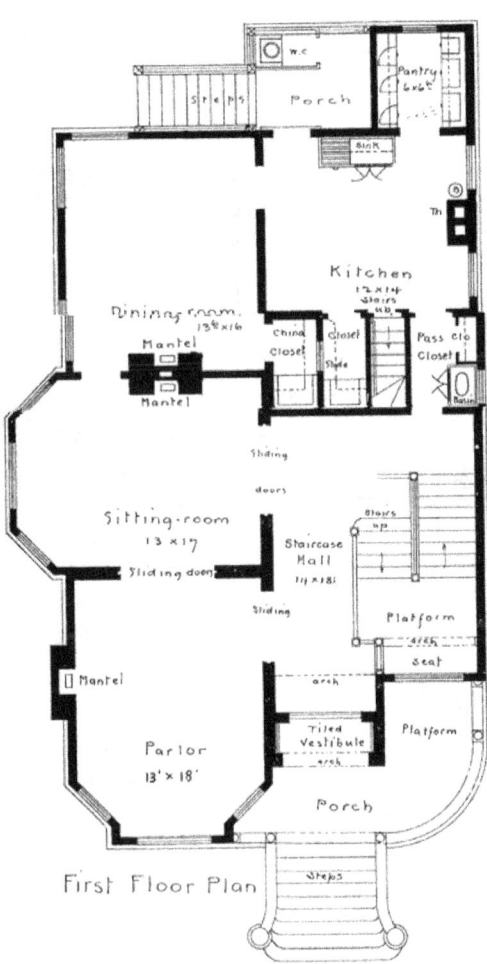

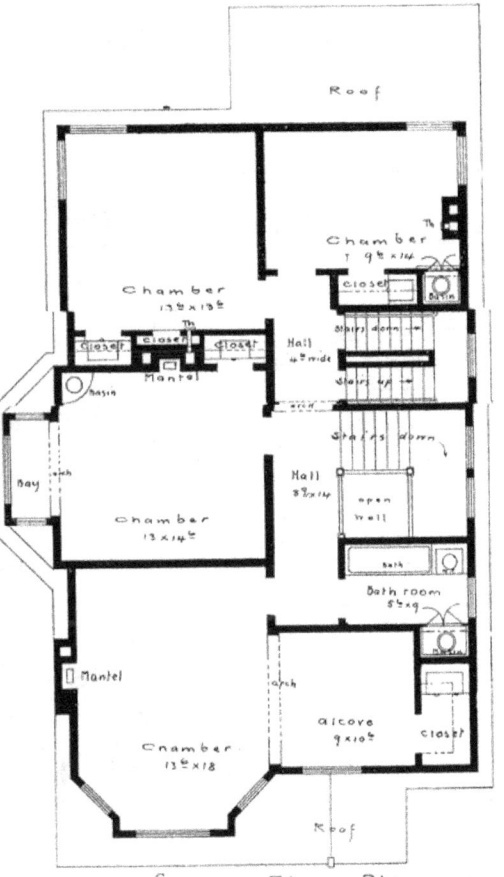

First Floor Plan

w.c.
Steps
Porch
Pantry 6×6'
Sink
Kitchen 12×14 with W.D.
Dining room 13'×16
Mantel
China Closet
Closet
Slide
Pass clo. Closet
Bath
Mantel
Sitting-room 13×17
Sliding doors
Sliding doors
Stairs up
Staircase Hall 14×18'
Platform
seat
arch
Mantel
Sliding
Platform
Tiled Vestibule
arch
Parlor 13'×18'
Porch
Steps

Second Floor Plan

Roof
Chamber 9½×14
closet
Bath rm
Chamber 13½×13½
Closet
Closet
Closet
Mantel
Hall 4' wide
Stairs down
Stairs up
arch
basin
Hall 8½×14
Stairs down
open hall
Bay
arch
Chamber 13×14½
bath
Bath room 5½×9
Mantel
arch
alcove 9×10½
closet
Chamber 13½×18
Roof

Scale 10 5 0 10 20 ft

Cost

Lumber	$900	Mantels	$250
Millwork	900	Labor	800
Brick work & Sewers	250	Cathedral Glass	75
Plastering	275	Bells &c.	30
Painting	250	Total	$4180.
Plumbing & Gas Fitting	275		
Hardware & nails	175		

ROSS VALLEY.

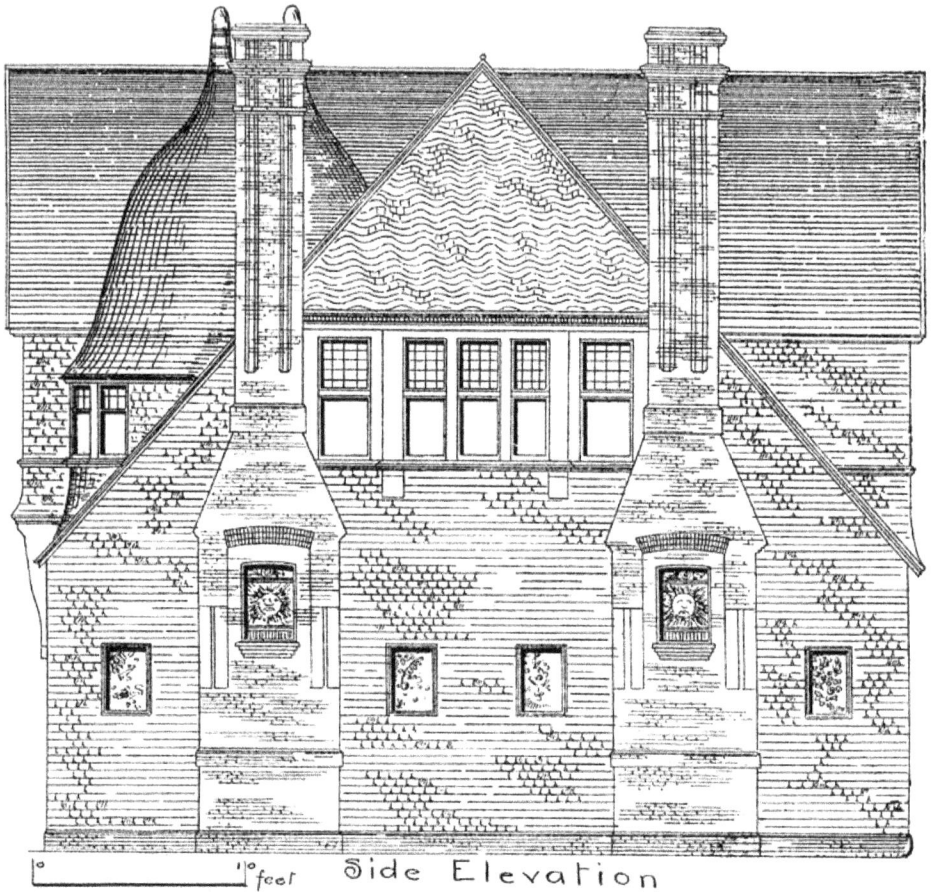

Side Elevation

A Summer Resort in extreme Knicker-
bocker Style. Exterior; Shingle effect
oiled and stained, Bell shaped tower,
Pressed Brick foundation and Outside Chimneys
with Cathedral Glass windows over Mantels.
Interior; The Hall as a large flower Bay
in front in Plate Glass. The Drawing room
off the Hall and the Hall are finished in
Redwood, put on diagonaly in panels, the ceiling has Redwood
Beams and plastered between, and the plaster is tinted in
Olive tints. The Kitchen is large so that it can be as a
Dining room. Off the Kitchen is the Scullery. Up stairs
the rooms are arranged for solid comfort and in a style
suitable for the most particular. Sam'l & Jos. C. Newsom. Architects.

Front Elevation feet

12'

feet 5 4 3 2 1 0 5 10 feet

Staircase Hall.

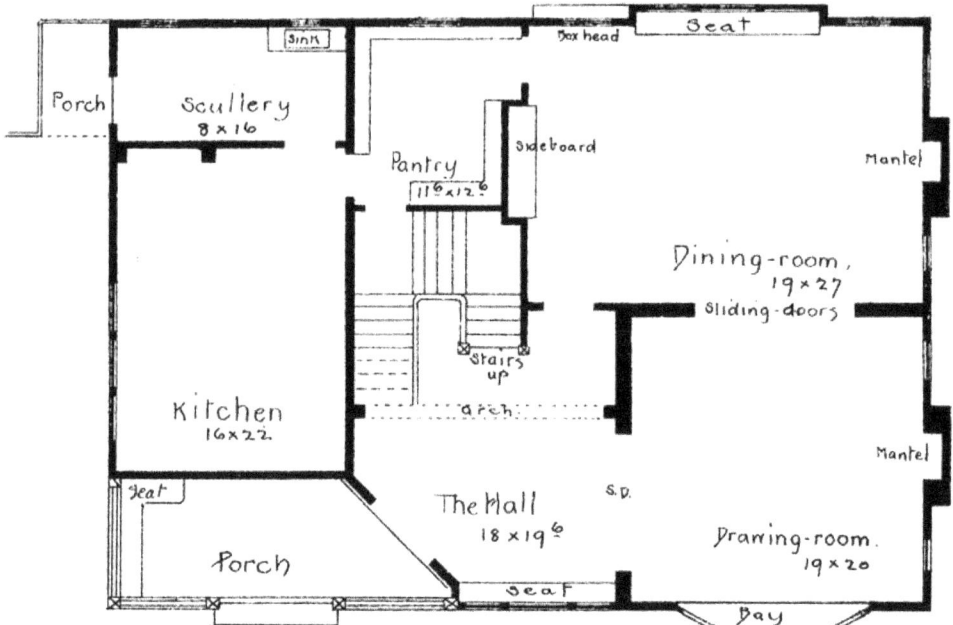

Porch

Scullery
8 × 16

Sink

Box head

Seat

Mantel

Pantry
11⁶ × 12⁶

Sideboard

Dining-room,
19 × 27
Sliding-doors

Stairs
up

Kitchen
16 × 22

arch

Mantel

Seat

The Hall
18 × 19⁶

S.D.

Porch

Drawing-room.
19 × 20

Seat

Bay

First Floor Plan

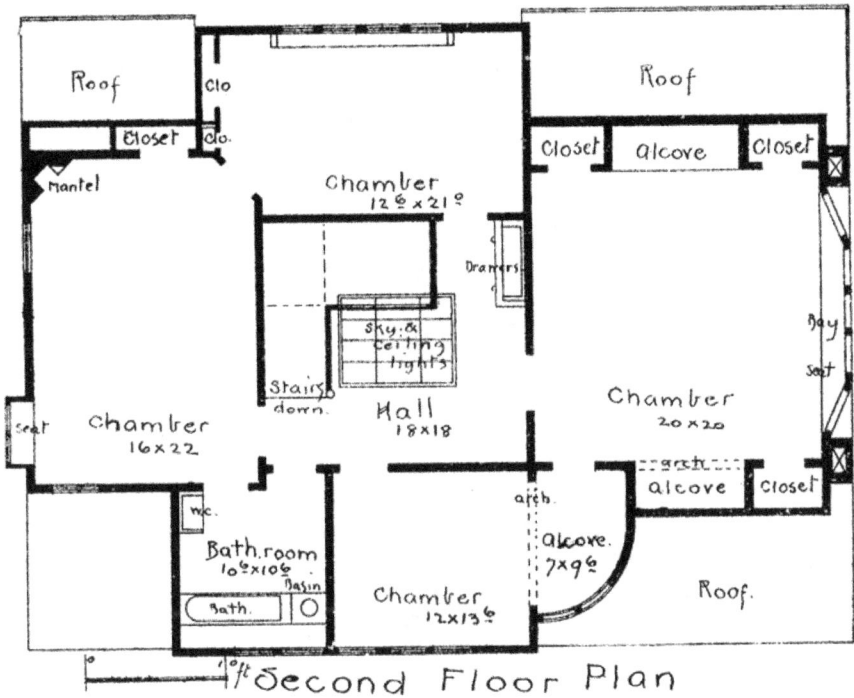

Roof

Clo

Closet

Clo.

Mantel

Chamber
12⁹ x 21⁹

Roof

Closet   Alcove   Closet

Bay

Seat

Drawers

Sky. &
ceiling
lights

Stairs
down.

Hall
18 x 18

Chamber
20 x 20

seat

Chamber
16 x 22

Alcove   Closet

w.c.

arch.

Bath. room
10⁹ x 10⁹

Basin

Alcove.
7 x 9⁹

Bath.

Chamber
12 x 13⁹

Roof.

1ᶠᵗ Second Floor Plan

Lumber	$ 1200	00	Hardware,	$ 200	00
Millwork	1100	00	Labor	1000	00
Brickwork. Sewers &c	350	00	Mantels	150	00
Plumbing. Tinning	----		Cathedral Glass	150	00
& Gas-fitting	400	00	Bells & Speaking Tubes	35	00
Painting	300	00	Hardwood floors &	----	
Plastering	350	00	Seats	200	00
			Total Cost	$ 5435	00

SAN RAFAEL.

Samuel & Jos. C. Newsom.

Architects. 504 Kearny St.

Top Floor. San Francisco.

Cost

Brickwork, Sewer	300
Lumber	400
Millwork Sash	
Doors, Blinds & Stair	1500
Labor	1100
Mantels	200
Plastering, Centers	400
Plumbing, Tinning	
& Bell Hanging	350
Painting	300
Cathedral Glass	150
Sundries	100
	$5300.

Front Elevation

ft.

Side Elevation

Chamber Mantel

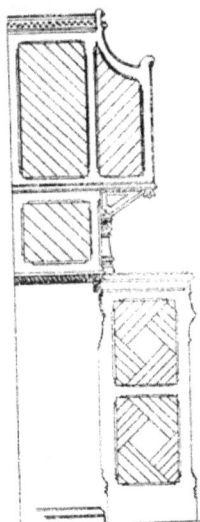

Dining-room Mantel

Balcony Bay. China
Closet

Pantry
5⁶x8⁶

sH

Porch
9x9

Steps

Boiler

Mantel Range

Dining-room
16x17⁶

Kitchen
13x14⁶

arch

Platform

Stairs
up Hall
8x5⁶

Porch

Steps

Stairs
up

Staircase Hall
18x20.

w.c
Lavatory
5⁶x7

Mantel

Sliding doors

arch.

Hall
7x10

Mantel.

Bay

Reception
Hall.
9x12

seat

Parlor
15x21

Porch.

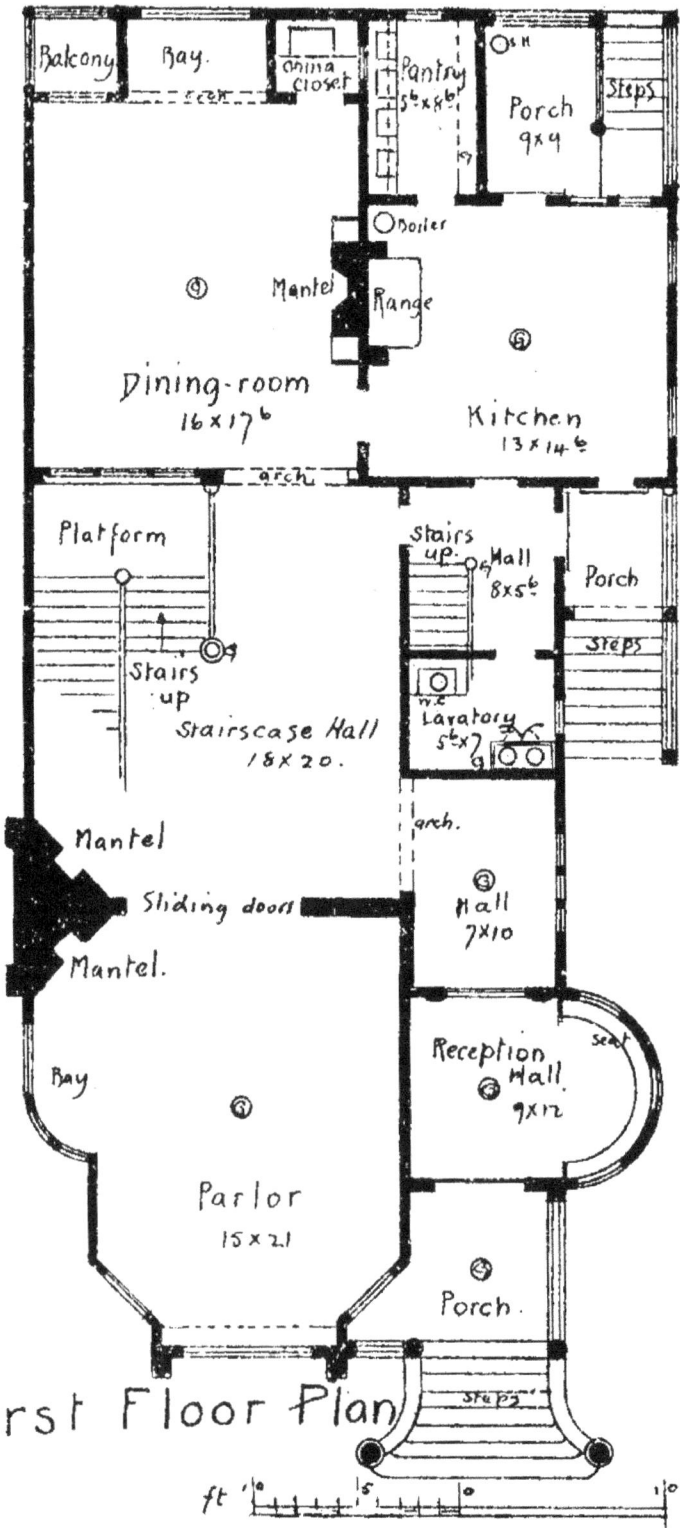

First Floor Plan

ft
5
10

Chamber
16 × 21⁶

Chamber 11×14⁶
closet
Basin
Basin
closet

Closet
w.c Basin arch
Bath-room
9⁶×12⁶
w.c
Bath

Chamber
11×11⁶

Hall
7×9⁶
Stair up

Balcony

open well

stairs arch down

stairs down

Staircase Hall
10⁶×18

Basin
Dressing room
6×7

Mantel

Bay
3⁶×12

Chamber
15×17⁶

alcove
6⁶×17

arch Bay
4⁶

arch
Bay
5×10

Balcony

Roof.

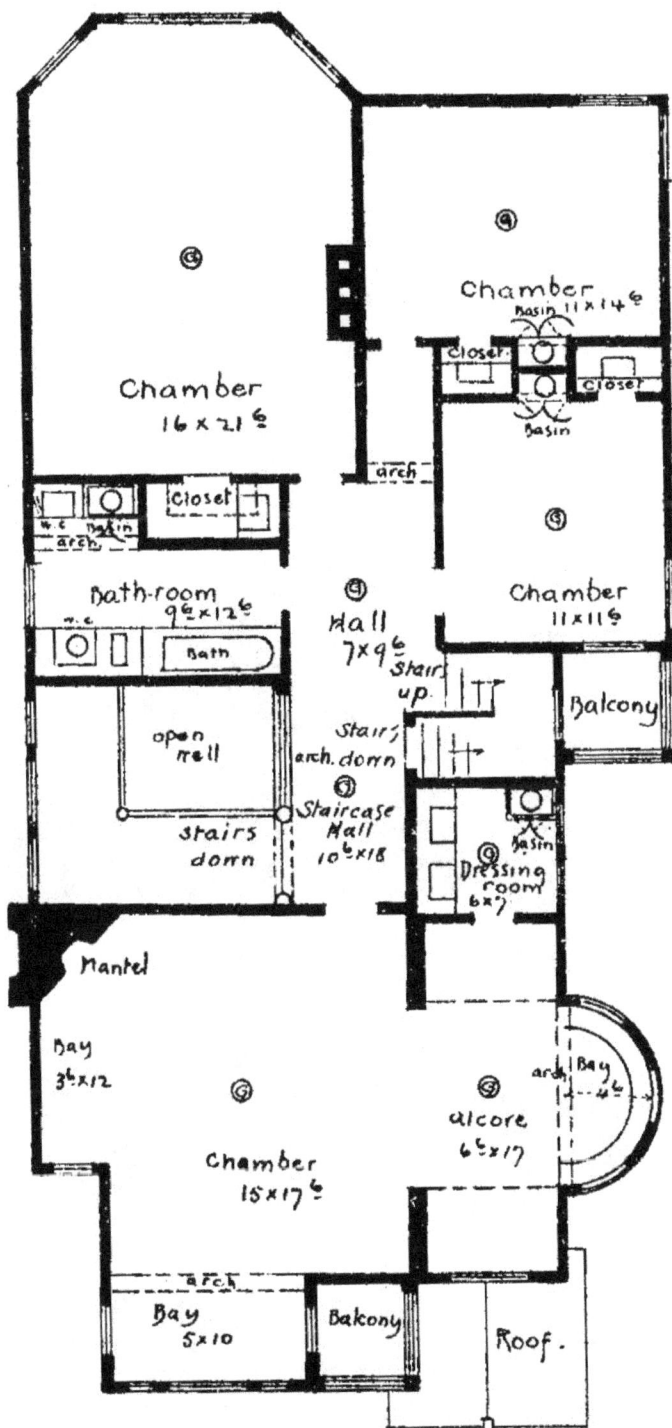

Second Floor Plan

0   10 ft

N.A.P.A.

A cheerful and substantial and economical Dwelling in the Free Style. The principal features are The Hall and Staircase there in. The Hall and Staircase and wainscotting will be built of Redwood and Burl Redwood panels, and cut and spindle filling to Arches, and over Stair Rail. Ash treads and risers Stained Glass windows in Staircase and Hall Directly opposite to Main Entrance as we

enter is a large open fire place heated by Gas Logs, with vent as shown. Redwood Mantel Tile Hearth, &c. Novel corner Circular End to Reception room. There being no Parlor and finishing over with Circular Bay. Sitting-room has Octagon End off Sitting-room is Conservatory connecting Sitting-room and Dining room making an interesting feature. The Dining-room is Octagon in shape, and is finished in Oregon Pine and Redwood put on diagonally Ceiling panelled in Redwood Floor of Oregon Pine with Herring Bone Border

Estimated Cost

Brickwork & Sewers	375
Lumber	800
Millwork (exclusive study)	1000
Glass and Stairs	
Labor	800
Hardware & nails	150
Cathedral Glass	75
Mantels	200
Plastering & centers	350
Plumbing & Tinning	350
Electric Bells & Tubing	50
Painting	300
Sundries	100
Total Cost	$4750

Front Elevation

Samuel & Joseph C. NEWSOM Architects. 504 Kearny St. San Francisco, Cal.

First Floor Plan

Steps

Pass Closet 5x7

Porch

Dining-room
Mantel 13x17½

China Closet

Conservatory 6x9

Clo.

Mantel.

Th.

Closet

Stairs up

Kitchen 11x16½

Closet

Pass Closet 6x6 stairs down

Clo

Pantry

Clo

Sitting-room 13x15

arch

Mantel gas logs

Stairs up

Mantel

The Hall 12x16

Reception-room 12x12

Seat

Clo

Vestibule

Porch

Steps

First Floor Plan

Bath-room 4'9x11

Bath

Closet

Boiler

Chamber 13'6x15

Chamber 11x13

Closet

Closet

Th

Roof

Hall 4'9x16

Hall

Stairs to attic

Stairs down

Chamber 10x13'6

Stairs down

Pass Closet

Closet

Closet

Hall 4'11 wide

Closet

Mantel

Chamber 14x15

arch
Bay 3'6"

Chamber 11x12'6

arch

Balcony

Second Floor Plan

NEWARK.

A cheerful, compact and convenient dwelling, this design embraces the advantages of the square form, and shows how such forms may be treated and dressed so as to have a variety of outline and picturesqueness of expression

The interior is conviently arranged The principal Hall is novel and interesting, it is entered through a brick Porch and is lighted by two windows of stained glass off the same is a Den furnished with seats and Patent Cloak Closets

Each of the principal rooms have open fireplaces

The exterior near the Front Entrance to the height of the Belt course of Second Story, is of Red Brick laid in Black Mortar

Estimated Cost

Brickwork, Sewers & Chimneys	300 -	Bells & Tubing	$15 -
Lumber	700 -	Hardware, Nails &c.	200 -
Millwork, Stairs & Glass	900 -	Mantels	200 -
Plumbing, Gas Fitting & Tinning	225 -	Cathedral Glass	50 -
Plastering	220 -	Labor	575 -
Painting	225 -	Total Cost	$3,610

Side Elevation

feet 5 10 20 feet

Section

Front Elevation

Elevation of Dining-room
showing Sideboard

In 1' 6" 0 1' 2' 3' 4' 5' 6' feet

STEPS

WINDOW HIGH UP
SIDE-BOARD

China
Closet

Slide
PANTRY

BIN BIN

PORCH

DINING-ROOM
12'-0" x 17'-0"

MANTEL

KITCHEN
10'-0" x 10'-9"
G

Boiler

M

MANTEL

G
Hall

STAIRS
UP

SINK

SITTING-ROOM
13'-0" x 14'-9"
B

SEAT

SEAT

ARCH

Stairs up

ENTRANCE HALL
12'-6" x 15'-6"

RECEPTION-ROOM
12'-0" x 12'-3"

Arch

Seat

Seat

DEN
6 x 8

C'l

Seat

MANTEL

MANTEL

Porch
7 x 8

Shelf

C'l

C'l

Seat

First Floor Plan

SEAT

CLOSET CLOSET

CHAMBER
11'-9" x 14'-0"

LINEN Clo.

CHAMBER
9'-3" x 11'-9"

MANTEL

MANTEL

W.B.

G

BATH-ROOM
6'-6" x 9'-8"

CHAMBER
13'-3" x 15'-6"

CLOSET

TUB

W.C.

ARCH

CLOSET

HALL
G

CHAMBER
13'-0" x 14'-0"

Stairs
down

MANTEL

MANTEL

CHAMBER
10'-0" x 13'-9"

BALCONY

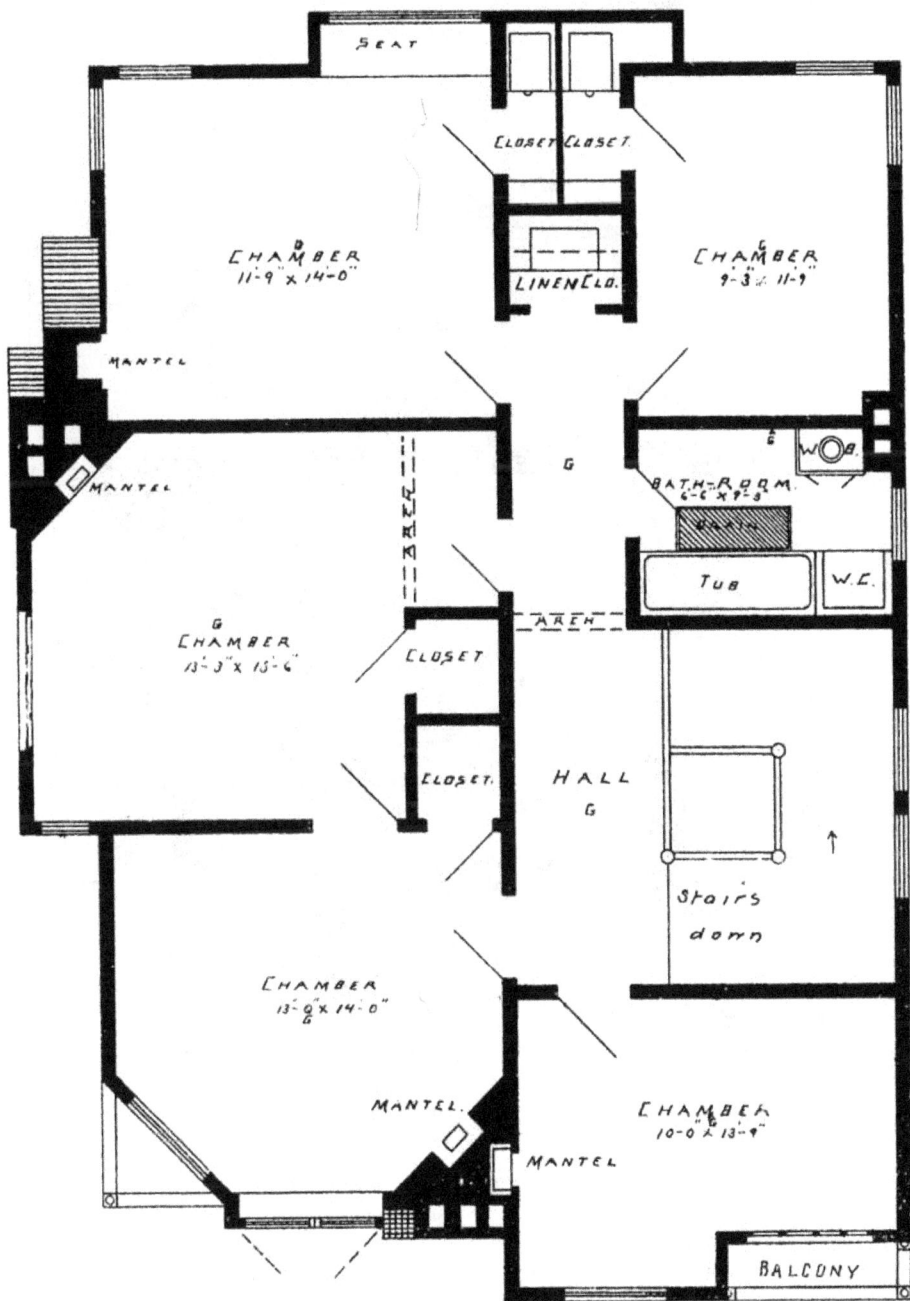

Second Floor Plan

feet 5 0 10 20 feet

FRUIT-VALE.

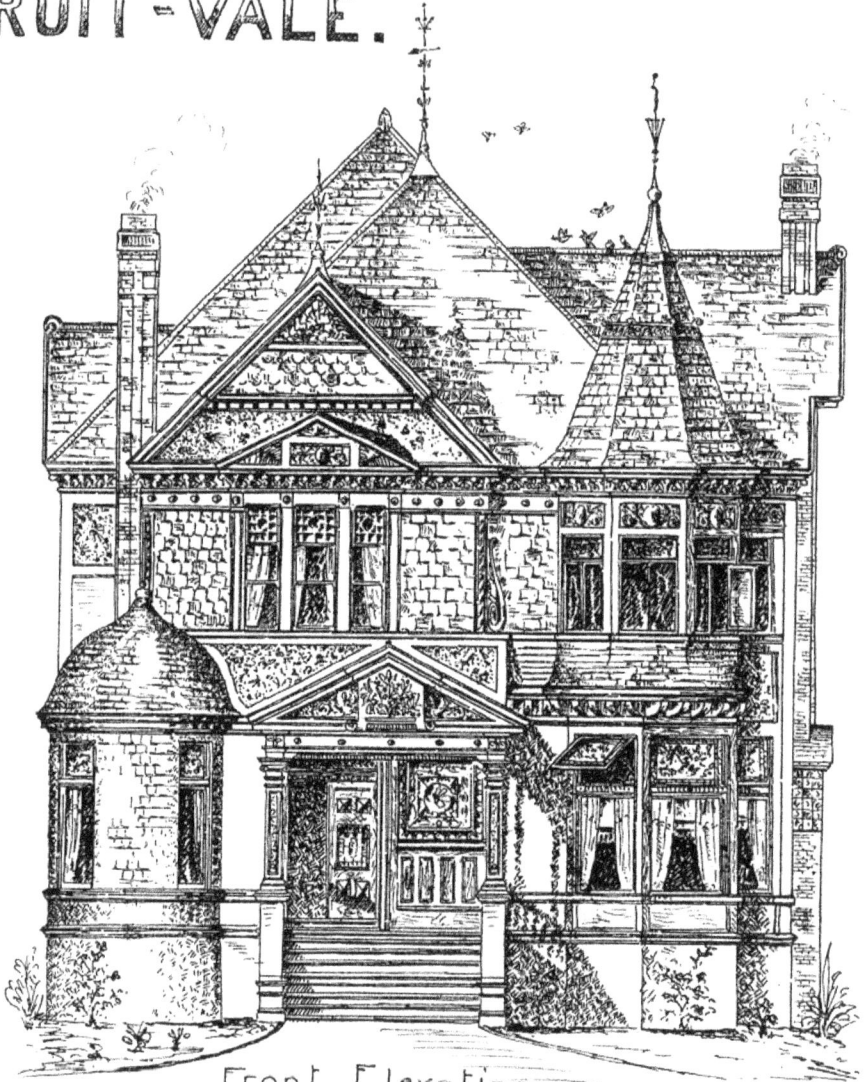

Front Elevation

Scale ^{10} 5   0   10   20 feet.

—cost—

Lumber	$1100
Millwork&sash)	1300
Doors & Glass)	
Plumbing & Tinning	350
Painting	300
Plastering & Brick work	400
Hardware & nails	250
Stained Glass	100
Labor	900
Sundries	300
Total	$5000.

The entrance of this dwelling leads into a spacious Hall with neat Staircase, arches and elaborate stained Glass windows. The Parlor, Sitting-room and Dining-room are on the South Side, with wide Sliding doors between each and into Hall. Second Story has 5 Chambers and Bath-room and Closets. The 1st Story is finished in Hardwood. Red Oak in Hall. Spanish Cedar in Parlor & Sitting room and antique Oak in Dining-room, the Kitchen in Pine

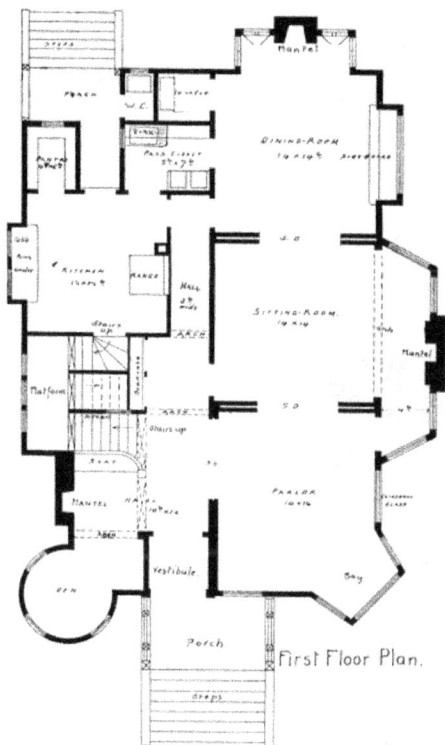

First Floor Plan.

Mantel

DINING-ROOM
14 × 14

Sitting-Room
14 × 14

Mantel

PARLOR
14 × 16

Porch

Kitchen

Hall

Vestibule

Bay

Steps

Dining room Bay

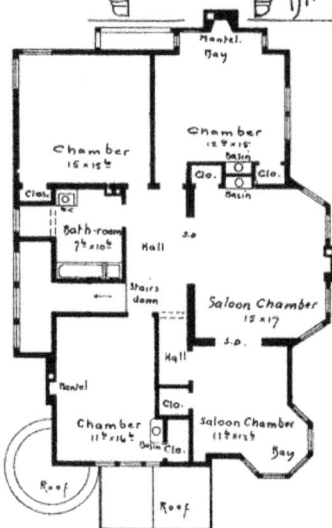

Second Floor Plan

Mantel. Bay

Chamber
15 × 15½

Chamber
12 × 15

Basin

Clo.

Clo.

Basin

Bath-room
7½ × 10½

Hall

Stairs down

Saloon Chamber
15 × 17

Mantel

Chamber
11½ × 16½

Clo.

Hall

Clo.

Saloon Chamber
11½ × 14

Bay

Roof

Roof

Samuel & Joseph C. NEWSOM
Architects
504 Kearny St.
San Francisco.
Cal.

LAKE MERRITT.

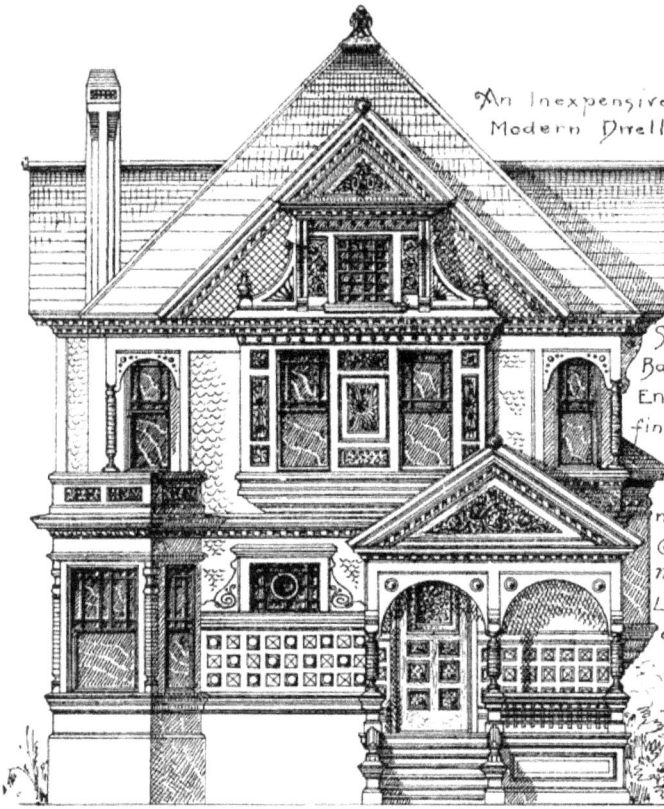

An Inexpensive and Tastey
Modern Dwelling of 8 rooms
with a Pleasant
Reception Hall,
easy and well designed
Staircase of Oregon
Ash. Corner Bays,
Outside Chimney
Secluded Den, Corner
Balconies, Large Closets
Entrance, and Vestibule
finished in Oregon Ash.
Interior –
Natural Red-
wood finish
Cathedral Staircase
Windows and Margin
Lights to balance
of House.
Spindle Arches,
Mantels of
Cherry.
Tiled

FRONT ELEVATION

Front Gable.

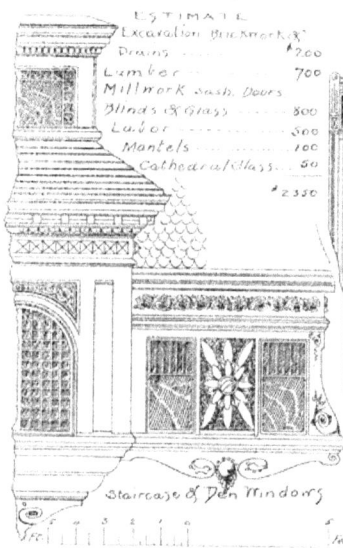

Staircase & Den Windows.

Front Door.

ESTIMATE

Excavation Brickwork		
Drains	$700	Bells & Hardware	$2350
Lumber	700	Plumbing & Tinning	125
Millwork Sash, Doors		Plastering Centers &c.	200
Blinds & Glass	800	Painting	240
Labor	500	Sundries	225
Mantels	100	Total Cost	150
Cathedral Glass	50		$3290
	$2350		

Samuel & Jos Newsom
ARCHITECTS
504 Kearny St Cor Cal St
Third Floor
San Francisco
Cal

Fronts and Hearths
Best of Plumbing, Fullers
Plumbing Goods.

SIDE ELEVATION

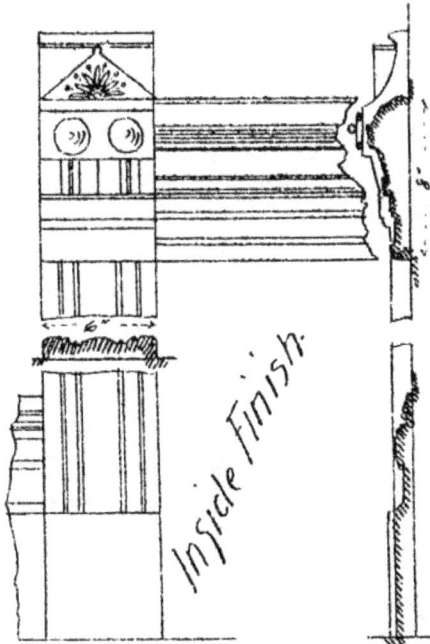

Inside Finish.

Laundry 6x9

Porch.

steps

Pantry
5x7

Servants
room.
7⁶x9

Closet

Pass Closet.
5⁶x9

Sink

Th.

Kitchen.
12⁶x14⁰

Mantel

s.p.

s.p.

Closet

Pass
Closet

Closet

Closet

s.p.

Dining·room
15⁶x16.

s.p.

Den
7x8

arch

Stairs
up.

platform

seat

Mantel

s.p.

Hall
9⁶x12⁶

Parlor
12⁶x17

Vestibule

Platform

arch

Bay

Porch.

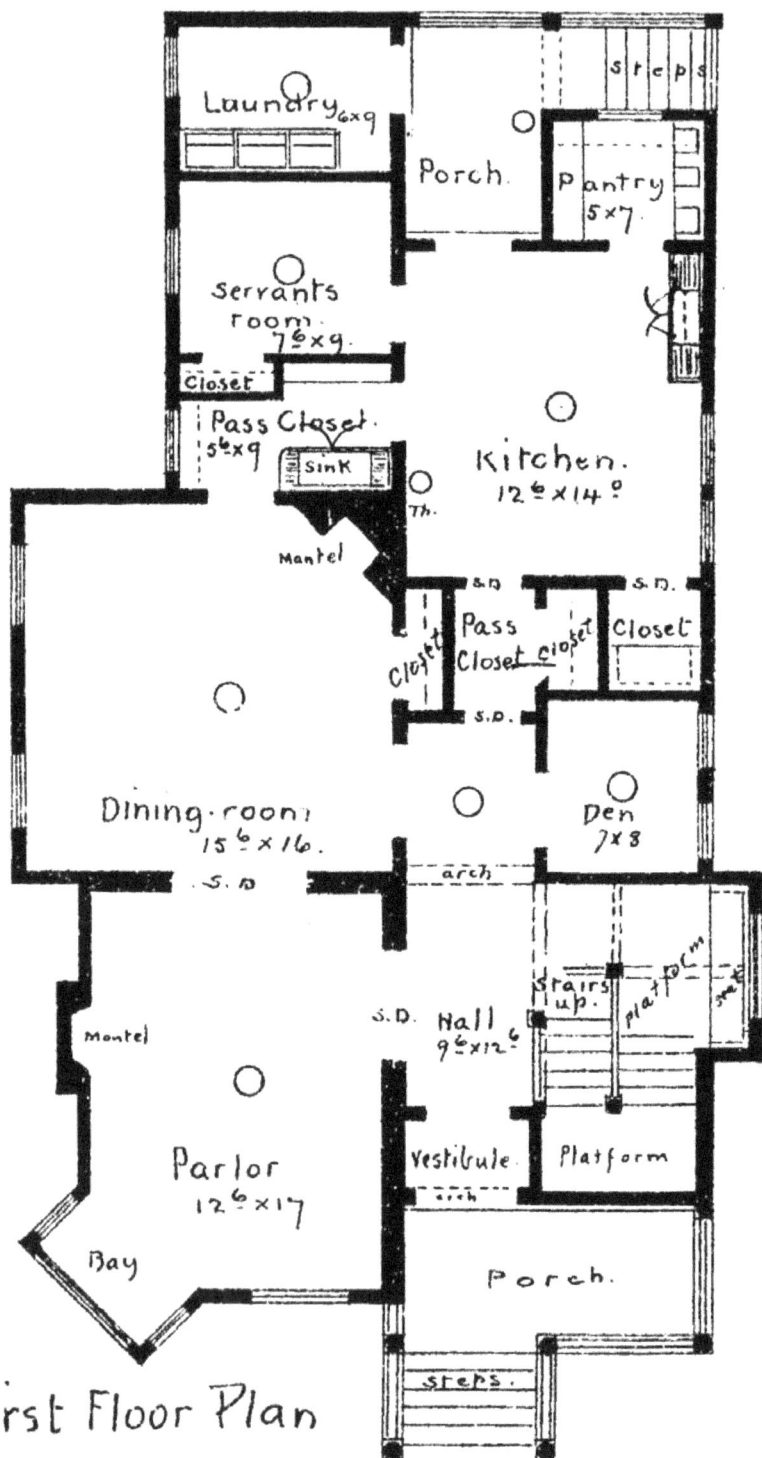

First Floor Plan

steps.

Ft   10   5   0

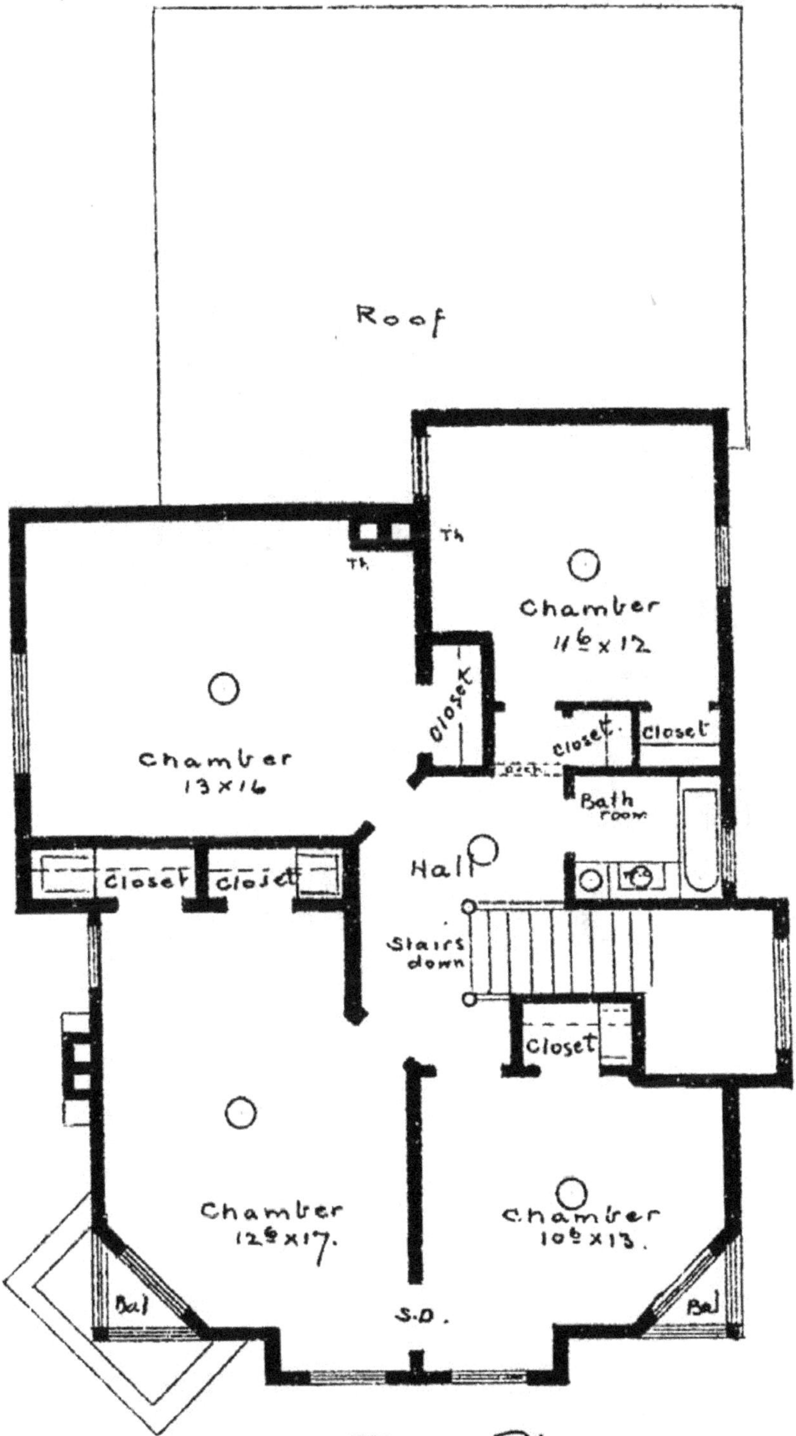

Roof

Th.
Th.

Chamber
11⁶×12

Closet

Chamber
13×16

Closet Closet

Closet Closet

Bath
room

Hall

Stairs
down

Closet

Chamber
12⁶×17.

c.hamber
10⁶×13.

Bal.

S.D.

Bal

Second Floor Plan

RICHMOND.

Section   Front Elevation

S.M. J.C. Newsom - Architects
San Aeming St. S.F.

Estimated Cost

Lumber	$800	Labor	$1800	
Millwork. Sash Doors & Blinds	900	Hardware	150	
		Mantels	200	
Plumbing & Tinning	400	Cathedral Glass	100	
Painting	250	Bells	50	
Plastering & Centers	350	Sundries	150	
Brickwork	250	Total Cost	$4400	

Excavation, Brickwork &
Drains ———————— $400
Lumber ———————— 1,000
Millwork Sash Doors, Blinds
& Glass ——————— 1,250
Labor ———————— 1,000
Mantels ——————— 150
Cathedral Glass ——— 100
Bells & Hardware ——— 225
Plumbing & Tinning —— 425
Plastering, Centers &c ——— 350
Painting ———————— 300
Sundries ——————— 100
Total Cost —————— $5290

This house has 9 rooms
and 2 in attic.   The Den, Hall,
Parlor and Dining-room have
polished floors, with Rugs in
center.   Mantels all of Cherry.
   Hall window is in antique
Cathedral Glass.
   Stair of Spanish Cedar
was built in the Western addition
San Francisco, with slight changes
Outside Pressed Brick Chimney
Terra Cotta Trimmings
Octagon Bay with Circular
Bay over -

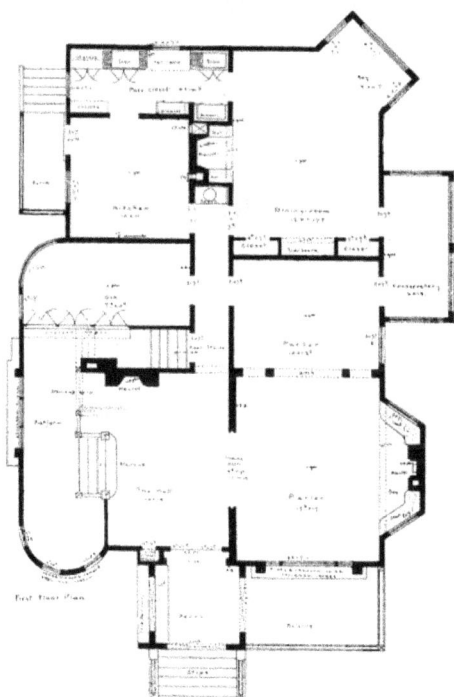

First Floor Plan

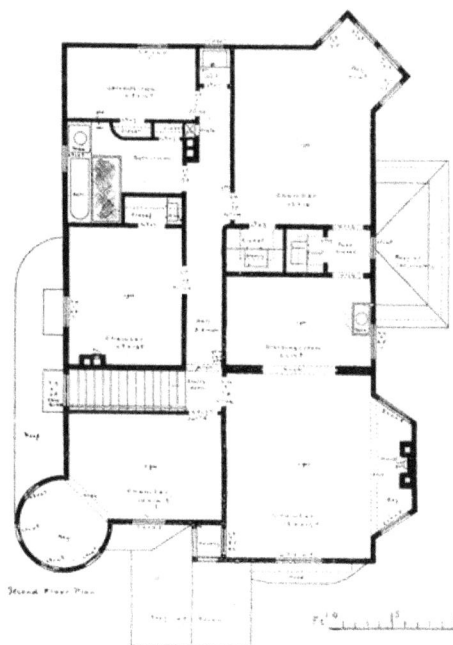

Second Floor Plan

WESTERN ADDITION

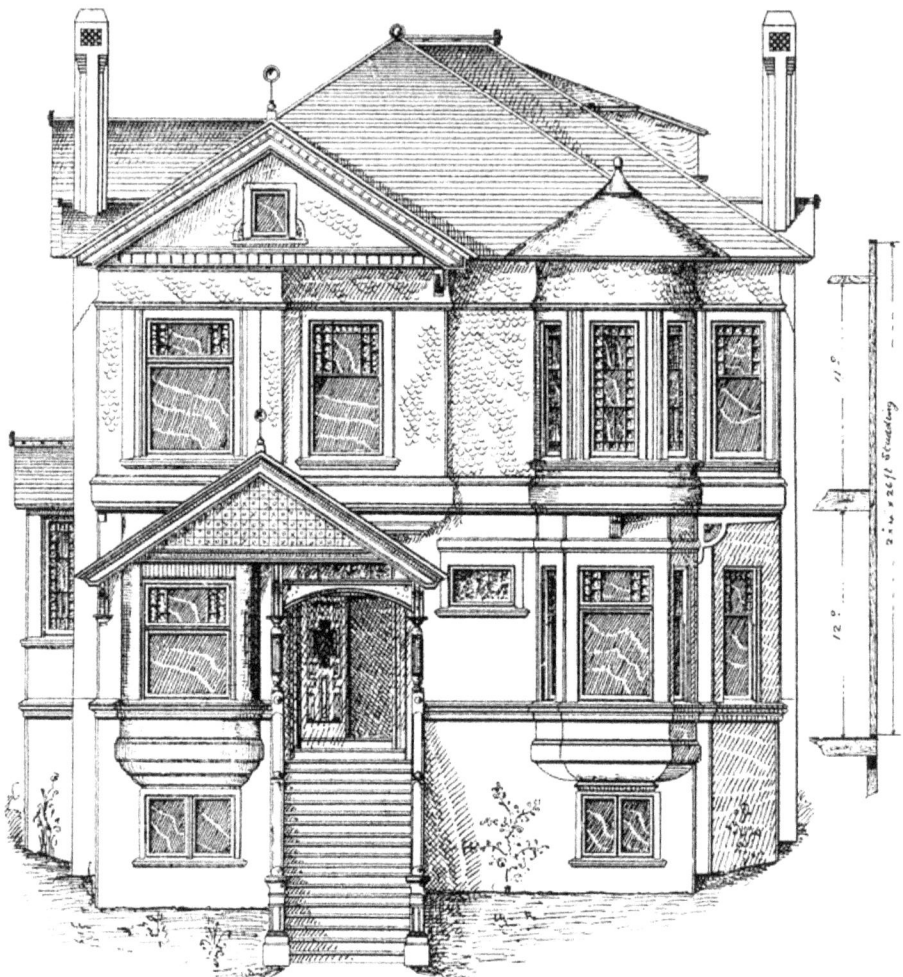

Front Elevation.

Excavation, Brickwork & Drains	$400
Lumber	1,000
Millwork Sash Doors Blinds & Glass	1,250
Labor	1,000
Mantels	150
Cathedral Glass	100
Bells & Hardware	225
Plumbing & Tinning	425
Plastering, Centers &c	350
Painting	300
Sundries	100
Total Cost	$5290

This house has 9 rooms and 2 in attic. The Den, Hall, Parlor and Dining-room have polished floors, with Rugs in center. Mantels all of Cherry.

Hall window is in Antique Cathedral Glass.

Stair of Spanish Cedar was built in the Western addition San Francisco. with slight changes Outside Pressed Brick Chimney Terra Cotta Trimmings Octagon Bay with Circular Bay over —

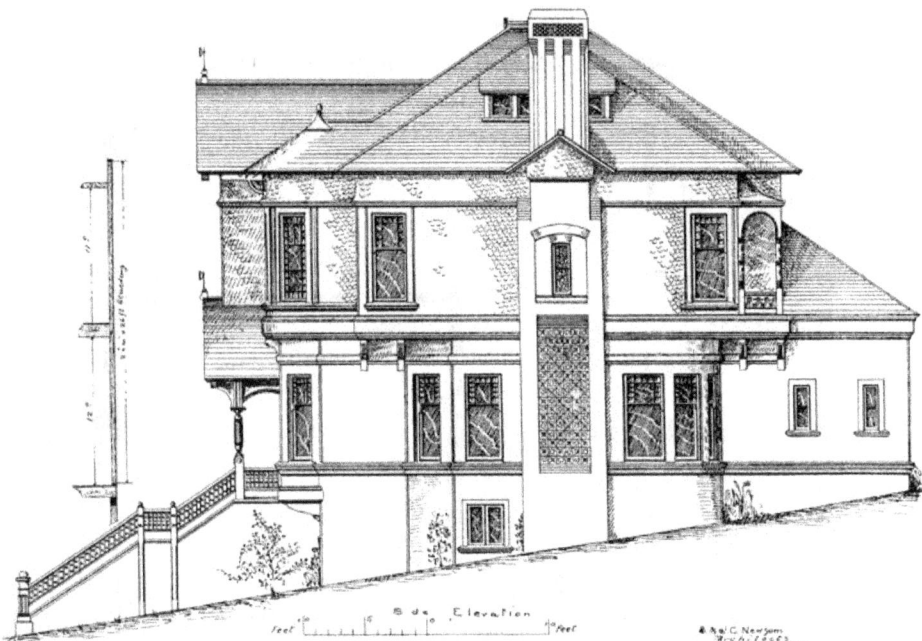

Side Elevation

Feet — 5' — 0' — 10' Feet

& Ne C. Newsom
Architects
804 Kearny St
S F

Elevation of Staircase.

Feet 5 4 3 2 1 0 5 Feet

Pantry

Bins

Porch.

Laundry

W C

Trays

Range

Sink

Pass Closet

China Closet

Kitchen
13⁶×14⁶

Back
Stairs

Closet

arch

Bay

Hall

Dining-room
14×17

Mantel

Closet

arch

Platform.

Spindle.

Glass
door

S. D

Mantel

arch

Bay

Stairs up.

S. D.

mantel

The Hall
16×16

Parlor
14×19

arch

Vestibule

arch

Bay.

Den
9×9⁶

Porch.

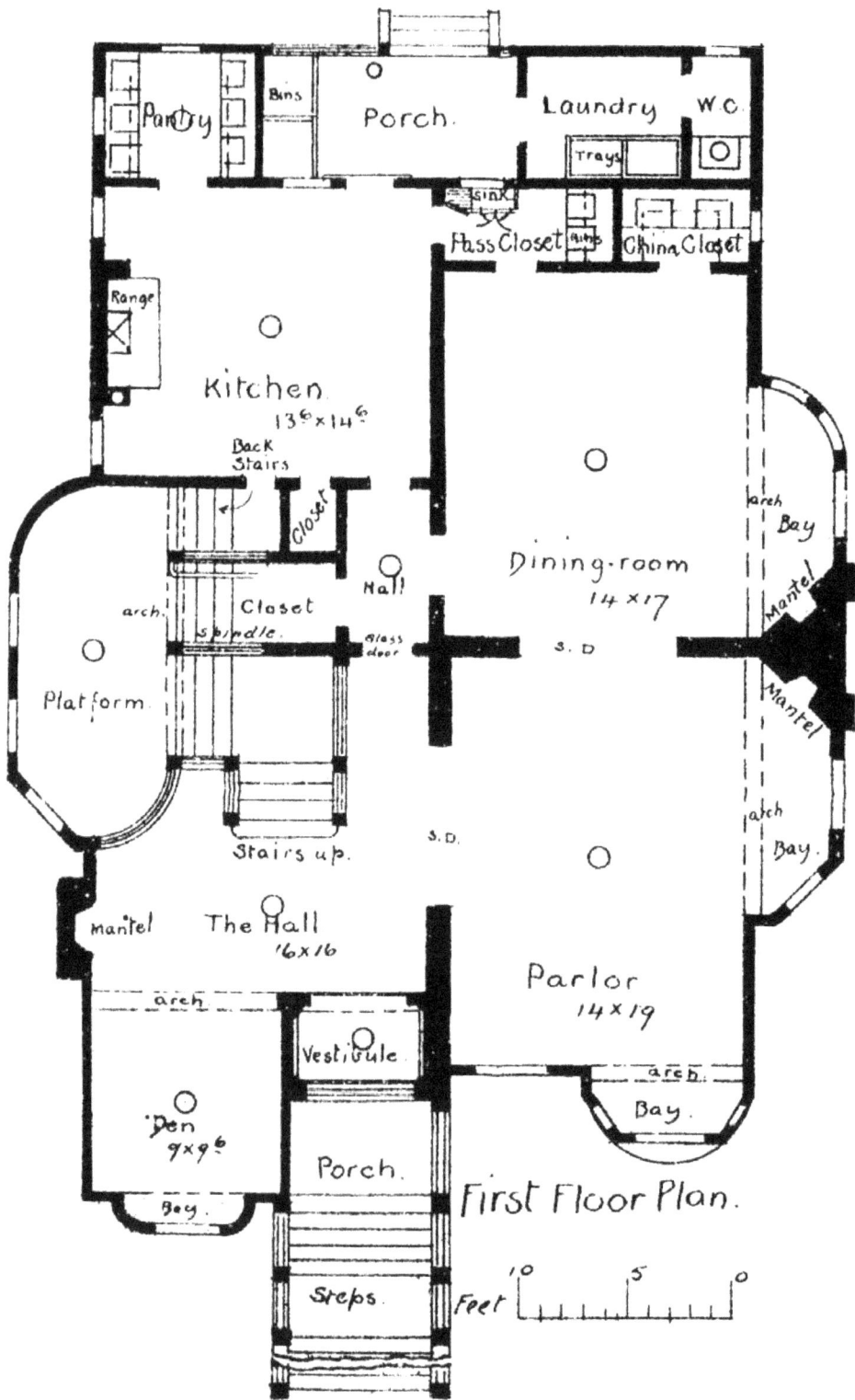

First Floor Plan.

Bay.

Steps.

Feet

10   5   0

Roof

Closet

Closet

Balcony

Chamber
10 x 12⁶

Closet

Chamber
13⁶ x 18

Mantel

To attic

Stairs
down

Bath
room

Dressing
Room

C't

Basin

C't

Mantel

Hall

Basin

Chamber
9 x 11⁶

Closet

Closet

Basin

Basin

arch.

7⁶ x 9

Chamber
13⁶ x 18

Closet

Chamber
9 x 14⁶

Bay.

Roof

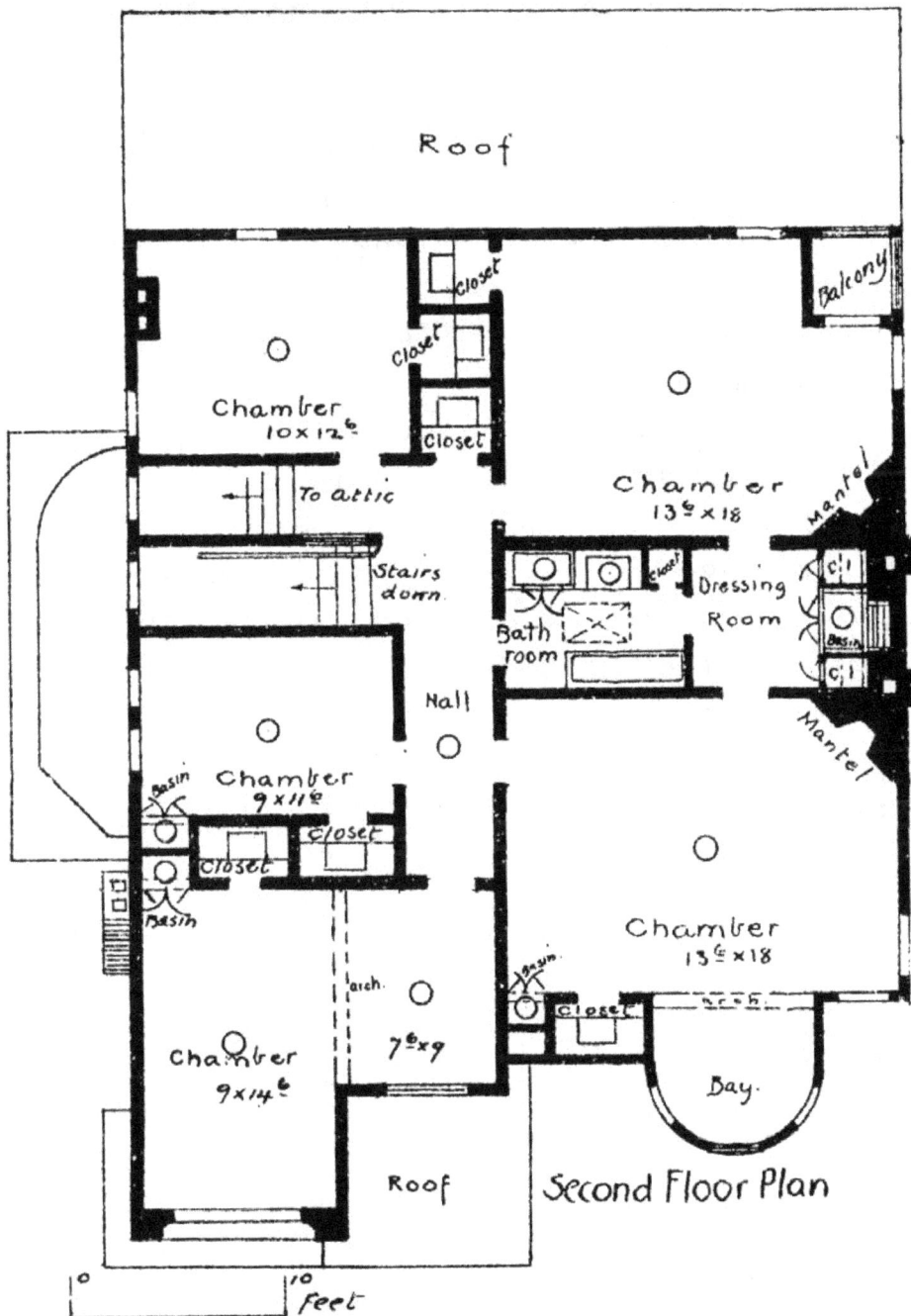

Second Floor Plan

0   10
Feet

SKAGGS SPRINGS.

Has 11 Rooms and all modern conveniences, Corner Entrance, Double Parlors
Recess Bays, Reception rooms, Large Hall
and Gas Log fireplace, easy and wide Staircase, Large Dining-room and Kitchen, Pantrys.
Closets &c in abundance. Second Story
has 5 nice and airy Bed-rooms. Closets
&c to each. Bath-room in a convenient
position. Recessed Balconies & Bays
 Exterior in the Free Style. Shingle and
Plaster affects and Terra Cotta Ornamental Belt Course, carved corners and center
panels, Gables Plastered. Tower Shingled
Outside Picked Brick Chimney. with Buff
Terra Cotta Ornaments

-> Estimated Cost <-

Lumber	$800.00
Millwork &c	800.00
Painting	250.00
Plastering	375.00
Plumbing. Gas Fitting & Tinning	350.00
Brick work & Sewers	300.00
Labor	700.00
Hardware, Nails &c	150.00
Cathedral Glass	130.00
Bells & Tubing	40.00
Iron work	20.00
Mantels	200.00
Total Cost	$4085.00

Scale

Front Elevation.

Side Elevation

Samuel & Jos. C Newsom
Architects
504 Kearny St
Cor. California St. Top Floor
San Francisco.
Cal.

ROOF

B.T

W.C

W.B

G
CHAMBER
11'0"x11'6"

G
HALL

CLOSET

CLOSET

ARCH

CLOSET

ARCH

CLOSET

G
CHAMBER
12'3"x18'0"

G
HALL
4'6"WIDE

G
CHAMBER
17'0"x13'0"

ARCH

ARCH

G. R.

G
HALL

G
CHAMBER
14'0"x16'0"

CLOSET

CLOSET

G
CHAMBER
15'6"x9'9"

B.H

B.H

BALCONY
5'6"WIDE

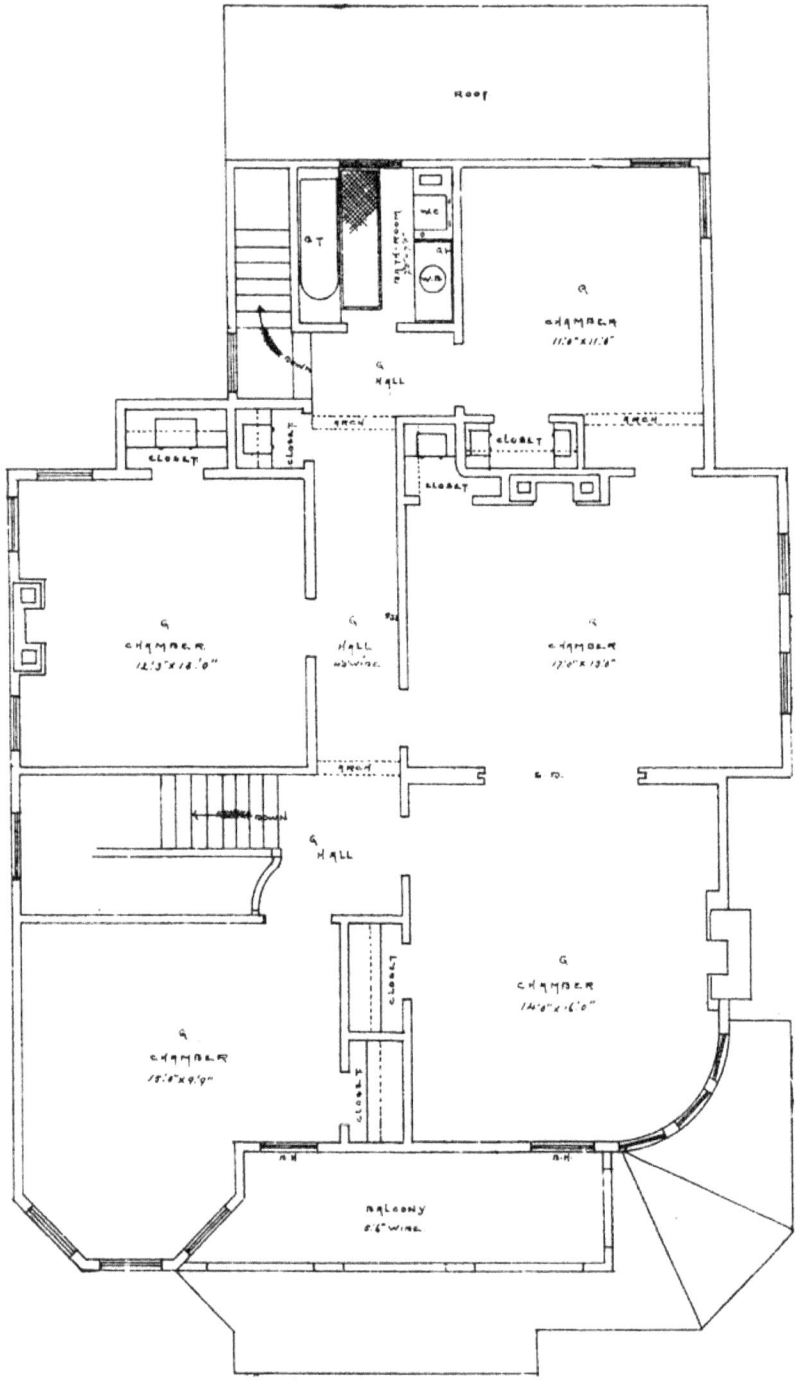

SECOND·FLOOR·PLAN.

Scale

10   5   0   10   20 feet

Closet   Closet

Mantel
and flue

Closet

Chamber
12⁶ × 14

×⁵

Chamber
12⁶ × 14

Balcony

×⁵

Stairs
down

×⁹

Hall
9 × 20⁶

open

Seat | hell

×⁹

×⁹

Chamber
13 × 14

Arch

Basin

Seat

Closet

Bay
2⁶ × 7

Mantel
and flue

Basin

Closet

arch

arch

×⁹

arch

Bath
room
6 × 10
×⁹

×⁹

seat

Bay

×⁵

Tub

Basin

Chamber
11⁶ × 17⁶

Chamber
12⁶ × 14

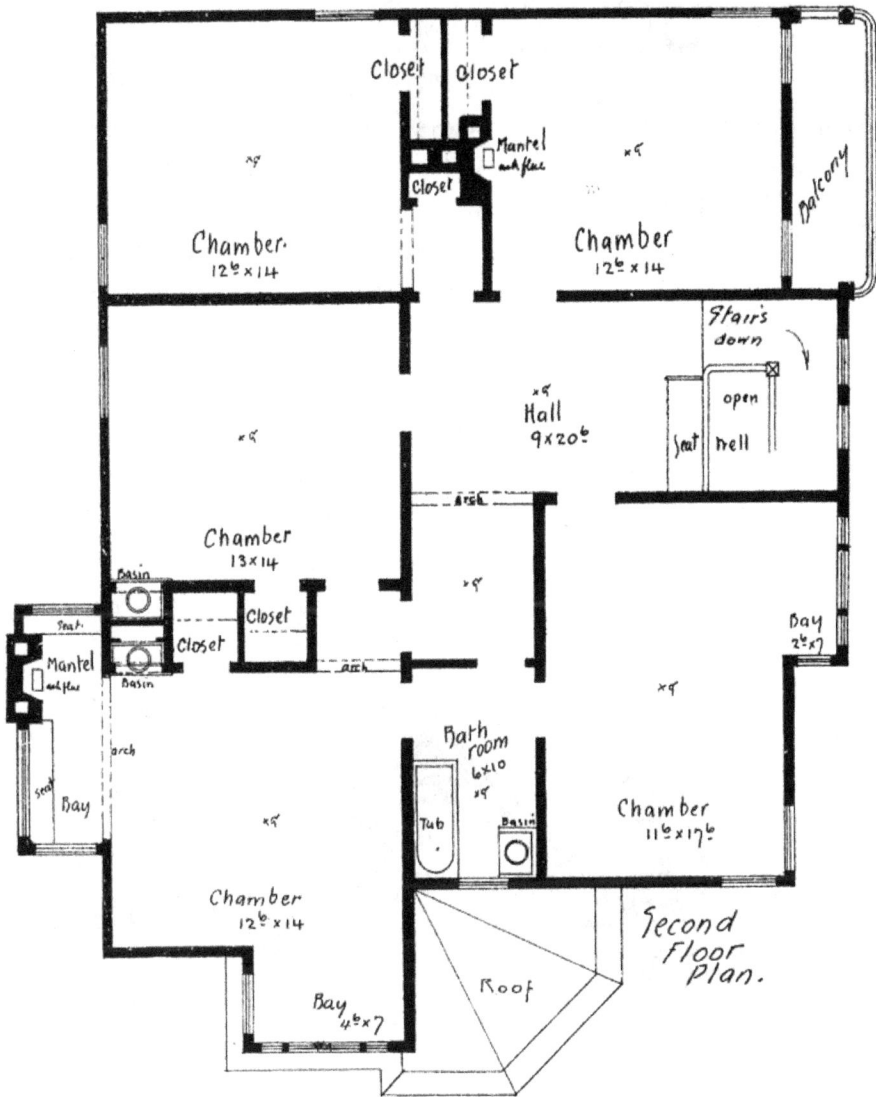

Second
Floor
Plan.

Bay
4⁶ × 7

Roof

STOCKTON.

Main features, The Front Part of Lower Hall is
connected so that the rooms can be thrown open
in case of a reception or other gathering, and off
The Hall is the Library in a secluded and isolated
position, just the place to spend a quiet time
There are both Front and Rear Stairs Large Closets and
plenty of them.

Front Elevation

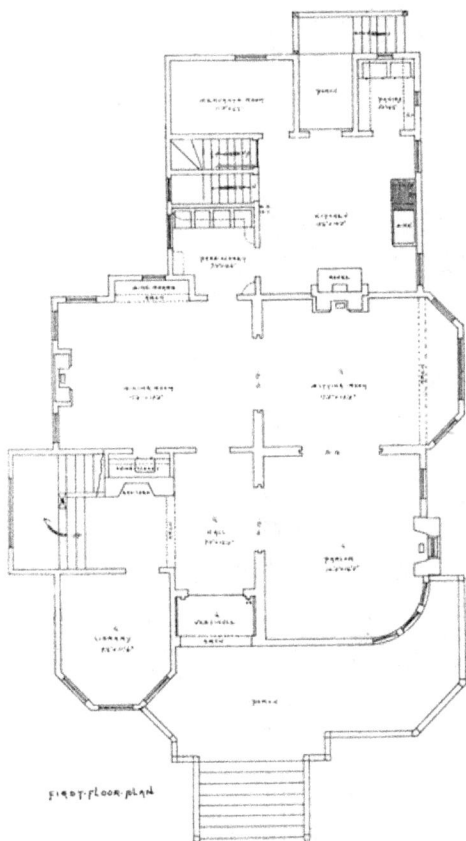

FIRST·FLOOR·PLAN

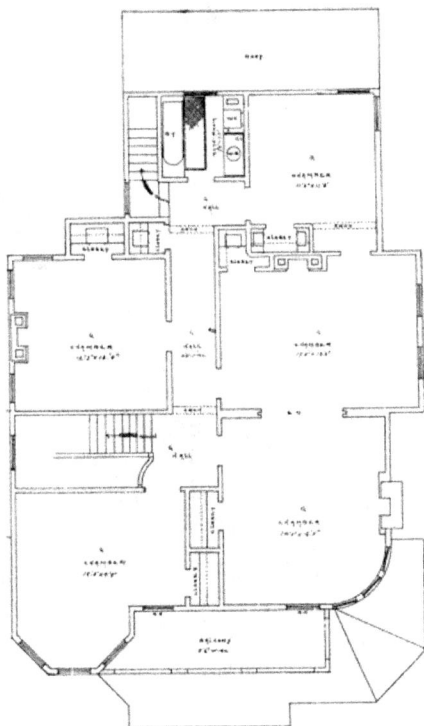

SECOND·FLOOR·PLAN

Estimated Cost.

Lumber	$900	Brickwork & Sewers	$250
Millwork, sash, doors & stairs	}1200	Cathedral Glass	100
		Bells & Tubing	20
Plumbing & Tinning	325	Labor	800
Plastering	350	Iron-work	20
Painting	275	Mantels	200
Hardware, nails &c	}150	Sundries	200
		Total Cost	$4790

The large Porch on both stories in Front makes this a desirable residence for a hot climate, and the arrangement gives a compact house for the amount of rooms, by this arrangement, rooms are got that would require a house of twice the size in the Old Style, five large Bed-rooms are got on the 2nd. floor with closets and Bath. The 1st. floor has six rooms all handy and arranged so as to furnish well.

Samuel & Jos C. Newsom. Architects
504 Kearny St. Top Floor
San Francisco. Cal.

VAN NESS AVENUE.

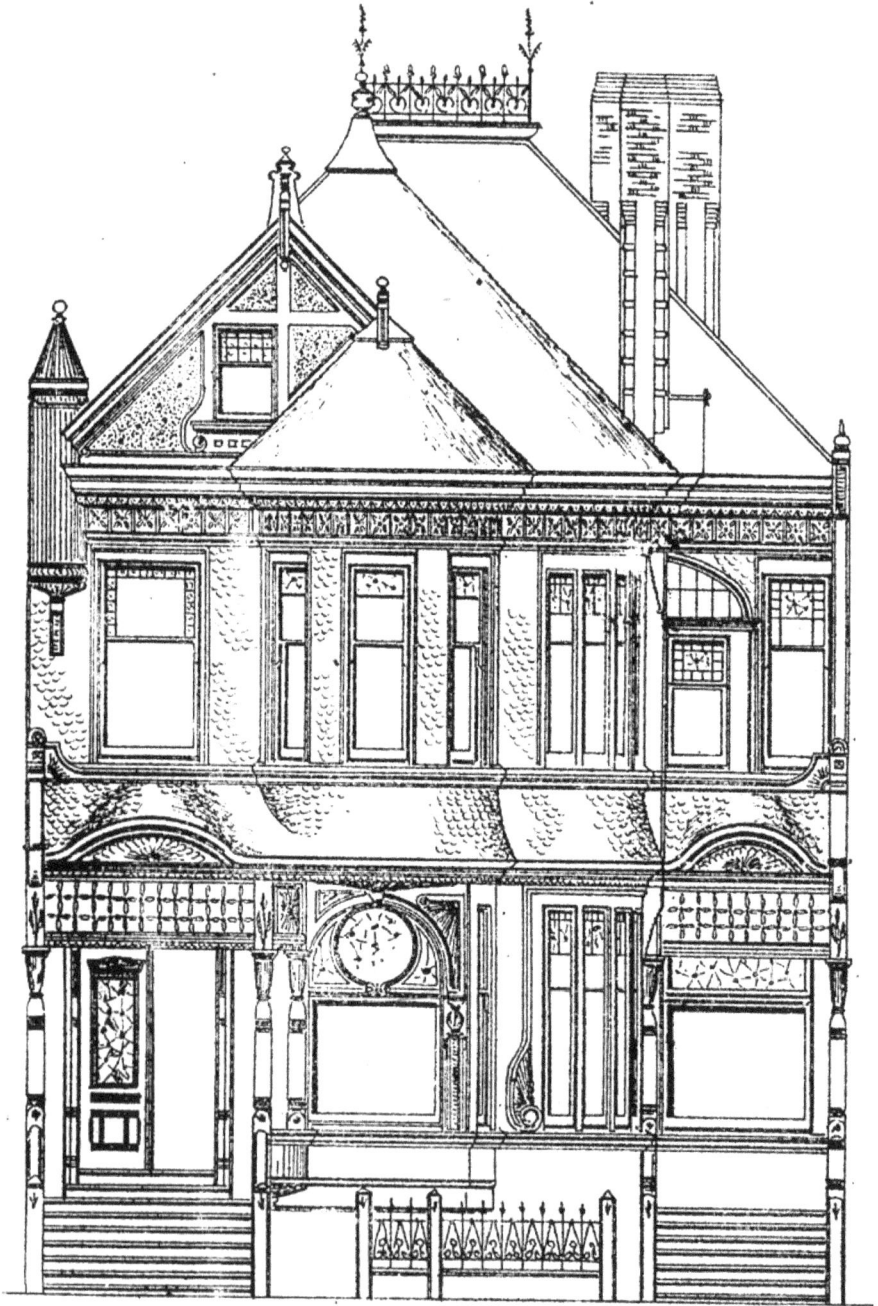

Front Elevation.

Scale 1 0   5   0   10 Feet

BERKELEY

Cost
Lumber — $350.00 Painting — 90.00 Total Cost $1490.00
Labor — 320.00 Hardware — 50.00
Millwork & Stairs — 385.00 Plastering & —
Plumbing — 75.00 Brickwork — 250.00

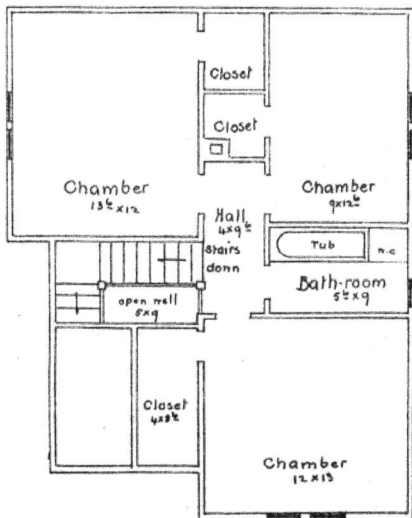

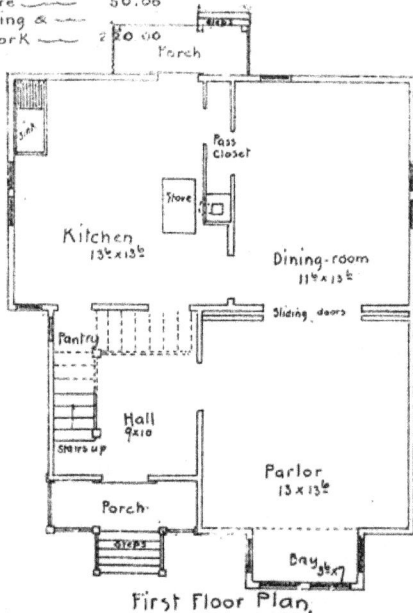

Second Floor Plan

Closet
Closet
Chamber 13½×12
Chamber 9×12½
Hall 4×9½
Stairs down
Tub
n.c
Bath-room 5½×9
open well 8×9
Closet 4×8½
Chamber 12×13

First Floor Plan

Porch
Pass Closet
Kitchen 13½×13½
Stove
Dining-room 11½×13½
Sliding doors
Pantry
Hall 9×10
Stairs up
Parlor 13×13½
Porch
Steps
Bay 3½×7

Side Elevation.

Estimated Cost

Excavation		$300.00
Lumber		1100.00
Millwork		1400.00
Labor		1100.00
Cath. Glass		100.00
Mantels, Bells &c. Hardware		545.00
Plumbing & Tinning		600.00
Plastering		450.00
Painting		300.00
Sundries		150.00
		$6045.00

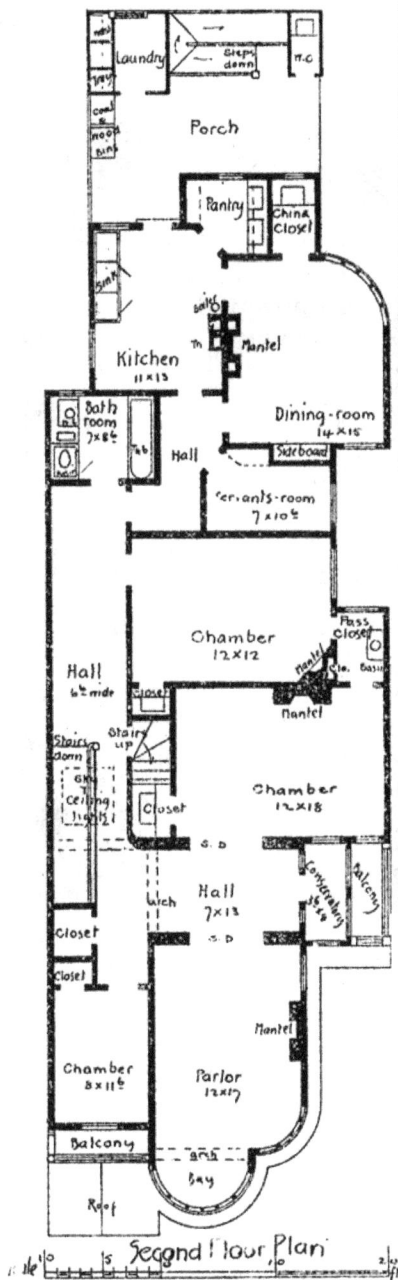

Second Floor Plan (left)

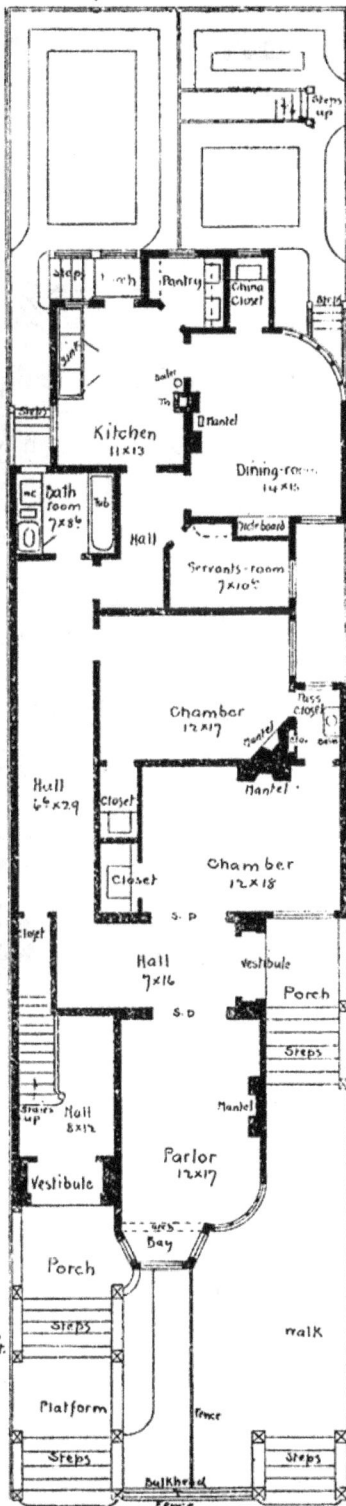

- Laundry
- Steps down
- w.c.
- coal / wood bins
- Porch
- Pantry
- China Closet
- Sink
- Kitchen 11×13
- Mantel
- Bath room 7×8½
- Tub
- Hall
- Dining-room 14×15
- Sideboard
- Servants-room 7×10½
- Chamber 12×12
- Pass Closet
- Mantel
- Basin
- Hall 6½ wide
- Closet
- Stairs down
- Stairs up
- 6ft ceiling light
- Closet
- Chamber 12×18
- S.D.
- Hall 7×13
- Conservatory
- Balcony
- S.D.
- Mantel
- Mantel
- Chamber 8×11½
- Parlor 12×17
- Balcony
- Bay
- Roof
- Bay

First Floor Plan (right)

- Steps up
- Porch
- Pantry
- China Closet
- Sink
- Kitchen 11×13
- Mantel
- Bath room 7×8½
- Tub
- Hall
- Dining-room 14×15
- Sideboard
- Servants-room 7×10½
- Chamber 12×17
- Pass Closet
- Mantel
- Basin
- Hall 6½×29
- Closet
- Closet
- Chamber 12×18
- S.D.
- Vestibule
- Porch
- Steps
- Hall 7×16
- S.D.
- Mantel
- Hall 8×12
- Stairs up
- Parlor 12×17
- Vestibule
- Porch
- Bay
- Steps
- Platform
- Fence
- Steps
- Bulkhead
- Fence
- Walk

Second Floor Plan

First Floor Plan

SAN FRANCISCO.

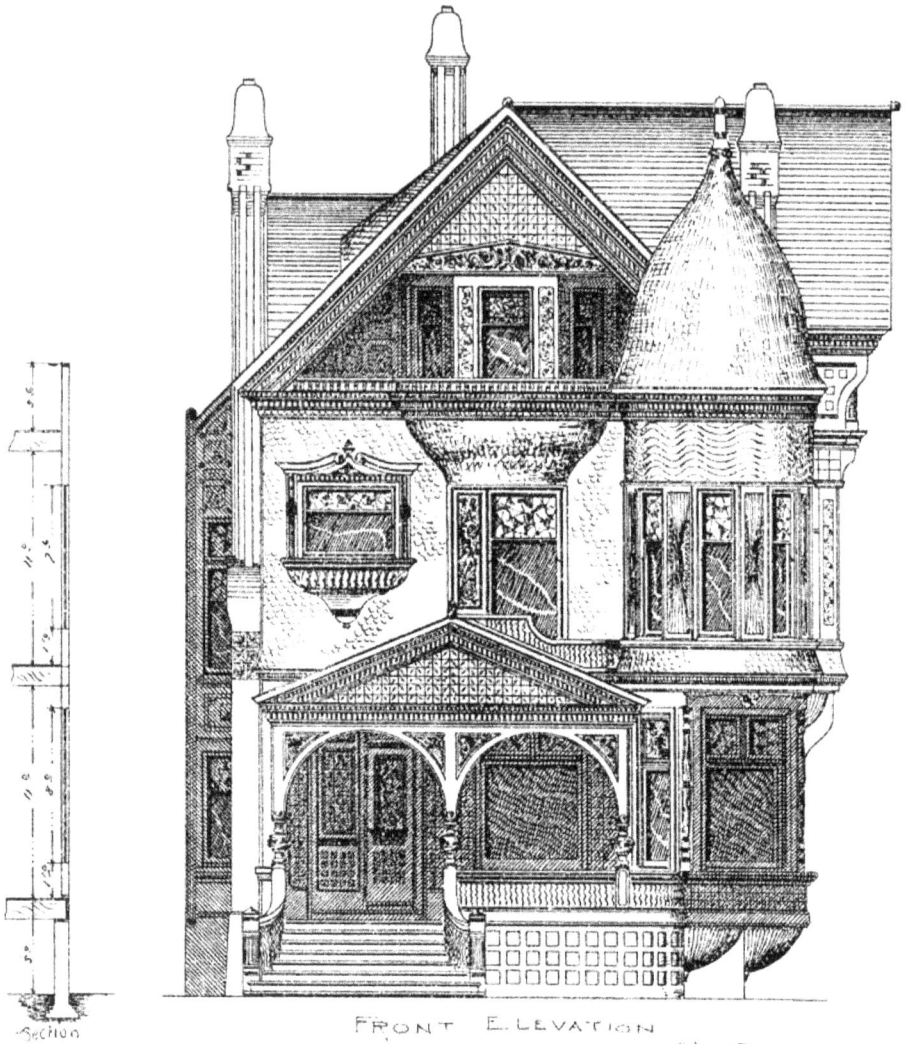

Section

FRONT ELEVATION

Scale 1'

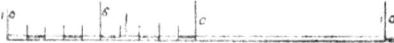

Samuel & Jos Newsom
ARCHITECTS
504 Kearny St.
cor California St.
Third Floor.
S.F.

This plate shows a City residence which can be built on a corner Lot 30 ft wide or an inside Lot 40 ft wide. The Hall, Parlor Sitting-room and Dining-room can be thrown together, while the Kitchen is in the rear away from the main part of house, under the Main Staircase is the Den or Library. The Front Hall as the usual Mantel and Screen in front of Stairs. Up stairs the front rooms are connected with Sliding doors and Spindle Arches, on this story the corner Bay in Front is Circular and square on Rear Chamber. In the Attic 4 or 5 rooms can be had for Servants rooms and Store rooms

Lumber	$1250
Mill work	2000
Brickwork	500
Sewers	150
Plastering	450
Painting	400
Plumbing & Tinning	600
Labor	1500
Mantels	400
Hardwood floors	200
Hardware & Nails	500
Cathedral Glass	200
Bells & Tubing	100
Sundries	300
Total Cost	$8550

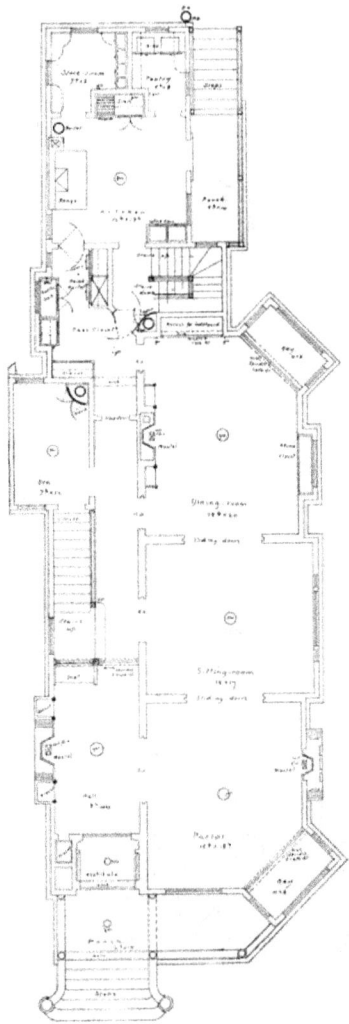

FIRST FLOOR PLAN

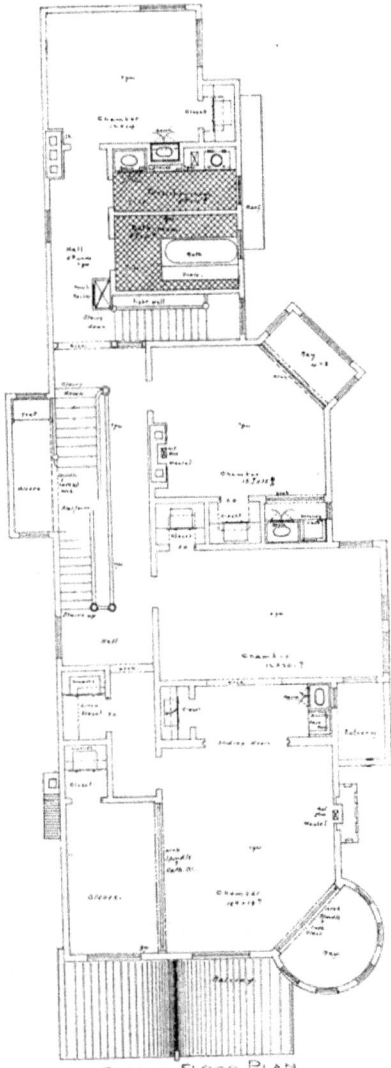

SECOND FLOOR PLAN

CALIFORNIA.

city house with 10 rooms and Bath. Laundry in Basement. Parlors are seperated by an arch and Columns, back of Parlors is the Dining-room-, on the right of Hall is the Study. On the 2nd Floor there are 5 bed-rooms, two of them saloon Bed-rooms, this plan has also given satisfaction in four different houses. The Style is Swiss Cottage.

Lumber	$1100
Millwork, Stairs & Sash	1400
Painting	400
Plumbing	450
Plastering	450
Brickwork	300
Hardware	250
Glass	200
Bells &c.	50
Mantels	300
Grading	100
Tinning	100
Labor	900

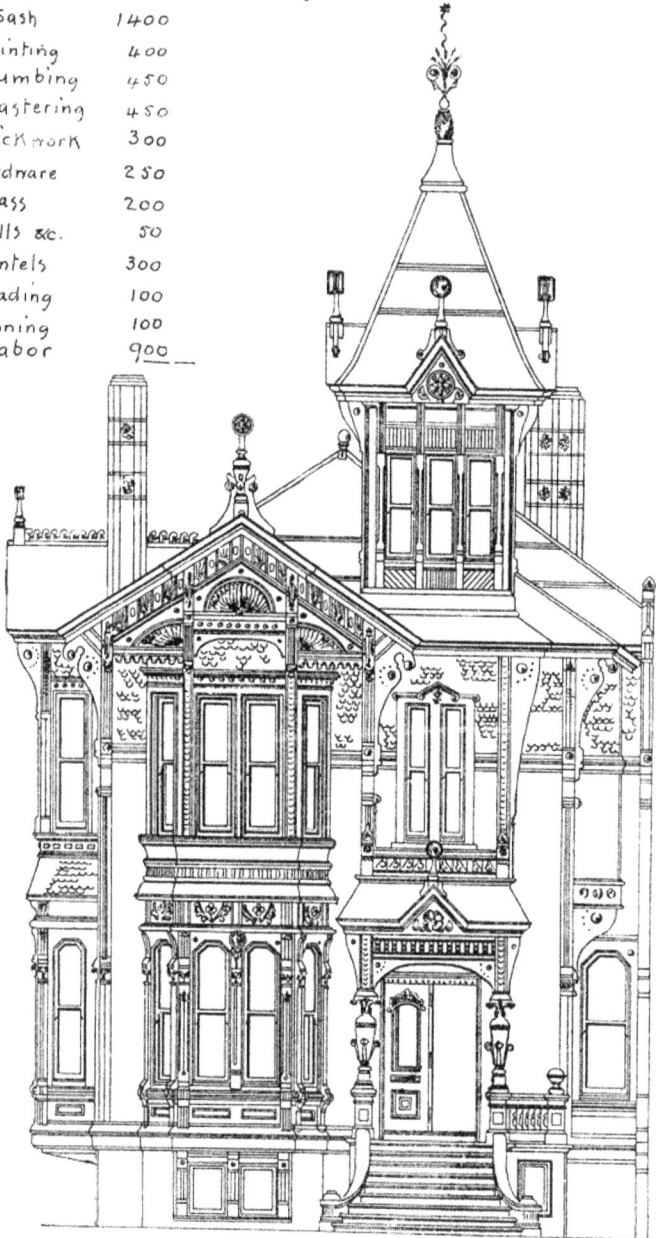

Total Cost $6000 =

FRONT ELEVATION

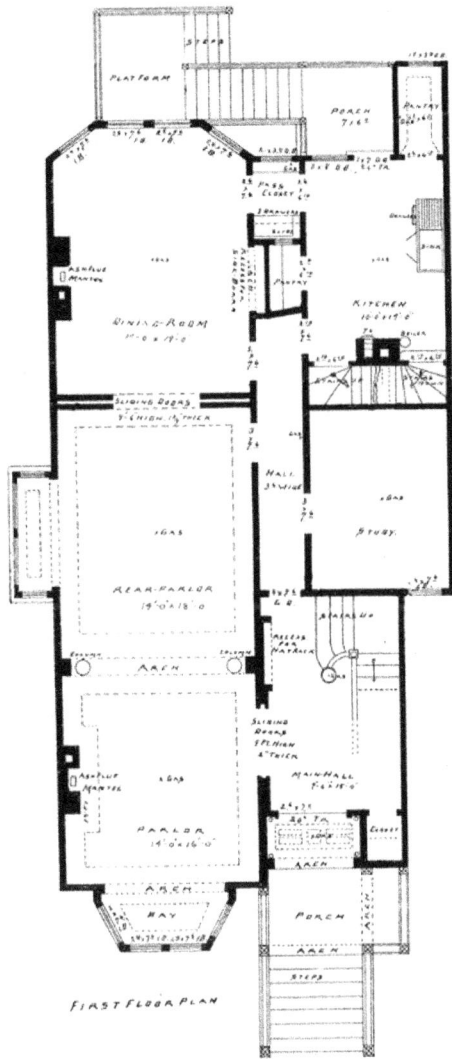

FIRST FLOOR PLAN

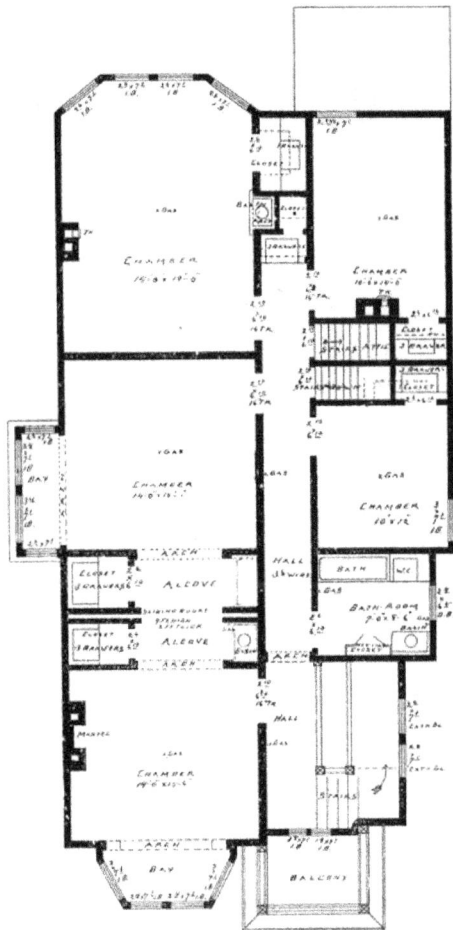

SECOND FLOOR PLAN

JACK HAYES CANYON.

A Suburban Residence with imposing Exterior and conveniently arranged Interior Exterior– The Main Entrance has a Moorish arch with Spindle filling, and Tower and Balcony above and Dormers on each side. Chimney Tops and Outside Chimneys of Pressed Brick and Cut Stone Trimmings Vestibule and Front Doors finished in Natural wood

Large Entrance Hall with Port Orford Cedar Stairs, finished natural, and fireplace with Brick Mantel, and Spindle Arch, and Sliding doors off each Side to Dining-room and Parlor, off Parlor connected by Spindle arch is Conservatory in Front, and by Sliding doors and Alcove in Rear is Sitting-room with Bay

The Dining-room is wainscotted 6ft high with Tile freize in same. Mantel recessed back and Bays or Alcoves on each side with Moorish arches. off Dining-room is Breakfast room, then Kitchen apartments in Rear. There are 7 Chambers up Stairs and Bathroom conveniently arranged, with front and back Stairs up to same

Estimated Cost	
Brickwork Sewers	800.00
Labor	1,500.00
Millwork Sash, Doors)	
Blinds Glass & Stairs	1,500.00
Hardware. Nails &c	300.00
Mantels. & Tiles	600.00
Cathedral Glass.	200.00
Plastering.	600.00
Plumbing & Tin.	450.00
Painting	400.00
Electric Bells &) Speaking tubes)	75.00
Lumber	1,400.00
Total Cost	$7,825.00

FRONT ELEVATION

Bauerbusch
Architects

Laundry
7×9

Fuel
room

Porch

Porch

Clo Clo

Mantel

Pantry

Chamber
17×15

Clo

Chamber
16×15

Lavatory
5½×6

Dumb
Waiter

Clo

Kitchen
12×16

Hall

Mantel

Bay

Sitting-room
12×25

Hall

Clo

up

Breakfast
room
9×10

Porch

arch

arch

Mantel

China
Clo

arch

Bay

arch

Mantel

arch

Parlor
15×20

Hall
17×24

Dining-room
15×20

arch

up

Bay

arch

arch

Bay

Conservatory
10×15½

do

Vestibule

Clo

Bay

Porch

First Floor Plan

Scale   1'0   5   0   1'0   2'0   5'0 ft.

SAN JOSE.

a Residence in the Modern Queen Anne Style, has Drawing room and Sitting-room connected with Arch and Dining-room with Sliding doors. an imposing Front Entrance and large Hall with unique arranged Staircase with Gas Log Mantel under, and secluded Den and Library off Hall Kitchen, Pantrys, Store closets Servants-room and Laundry in Rear of house. Up Stairs there are 6 large judicious arranged Chambers, and two Bath rooms and Basins in each Chamber. Dumb waiter, Dust chute and all Modern conveniences Known up to date

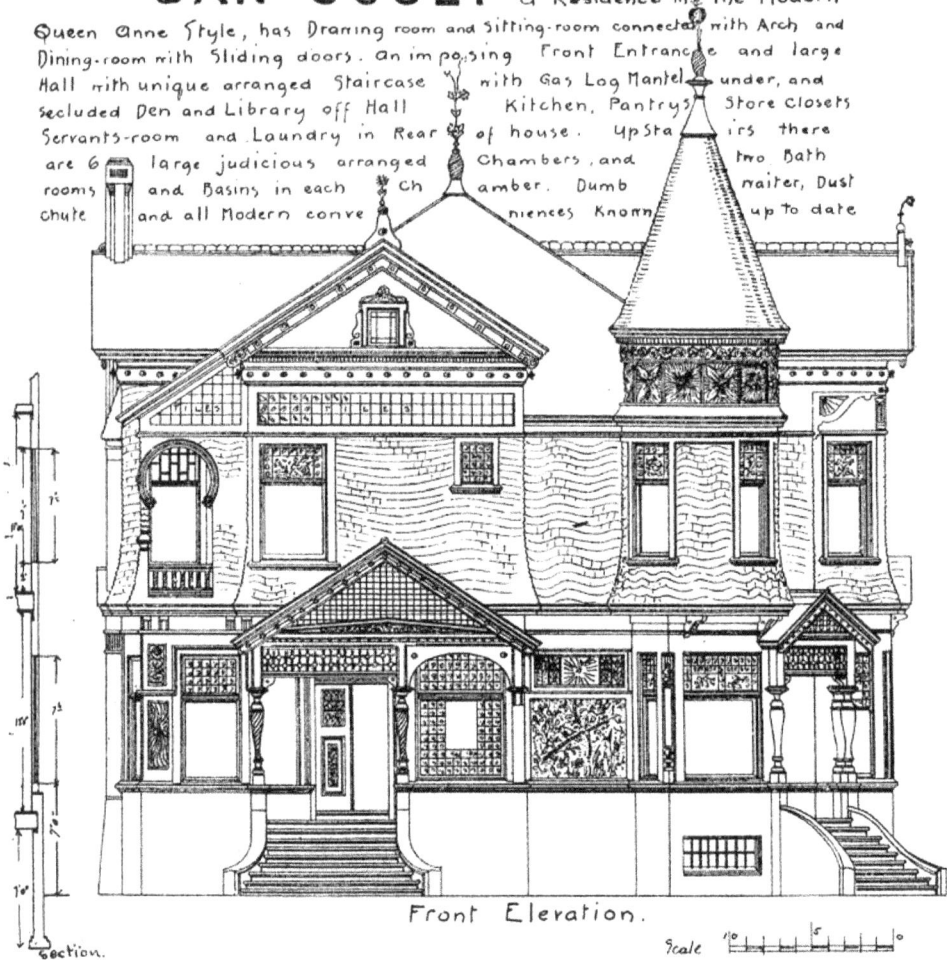

Front Elevation.

Section.

Scale

Estimated Cost

Lumber	$2000.00
Labor	1500.00
Millwork	2000.00
Plumbing	800.00
Plastering	700.00
Painting	500.00
Hardware	500.00
Iron Work	100.00
Cathedral Glass	600.00
Stairs	500.00
Brickwork	1200.00
Tinning	100.00
Tinting & Lining Interior	300.00
Mantels	500.00
Total Cost	$11.300.00

Side Elevation

Plaster Cornices & Centers

No.1
No.1
No.1
No.2
No.1
No.3
No.4
No.5
No.6
No.6
No.7
No.8
No.9
No.10
No.11
No.12
No.13
No.13
No.14
No.15

Samuel & Co, C. Kerr &c.
Architect's S.F.
504 Kearny.
Top Floor
S.F.

Steps

Pantry

Porch

Laundry
8x13

B

Store-room

Ramp

Kitchen

Servants room

Sink

Stair up

W.c.

Porch

Steps

Pantry

Slide

China closet

Shelves

Rear Hall

Basin

Mantel

Mantel

Sliding doors

Dining-room
13x23⁶

arch

Bay

Closet

Sitting-room
14x17⁶

arch

Mantel

Platform

Stairs up

arch

Verandah

arch

Main Hall

Den
9x11⁹

arch

Sliding doors

Drawing-room

Vestibule

Bay

Steps

Porch

Library
6⁶x10

Steps

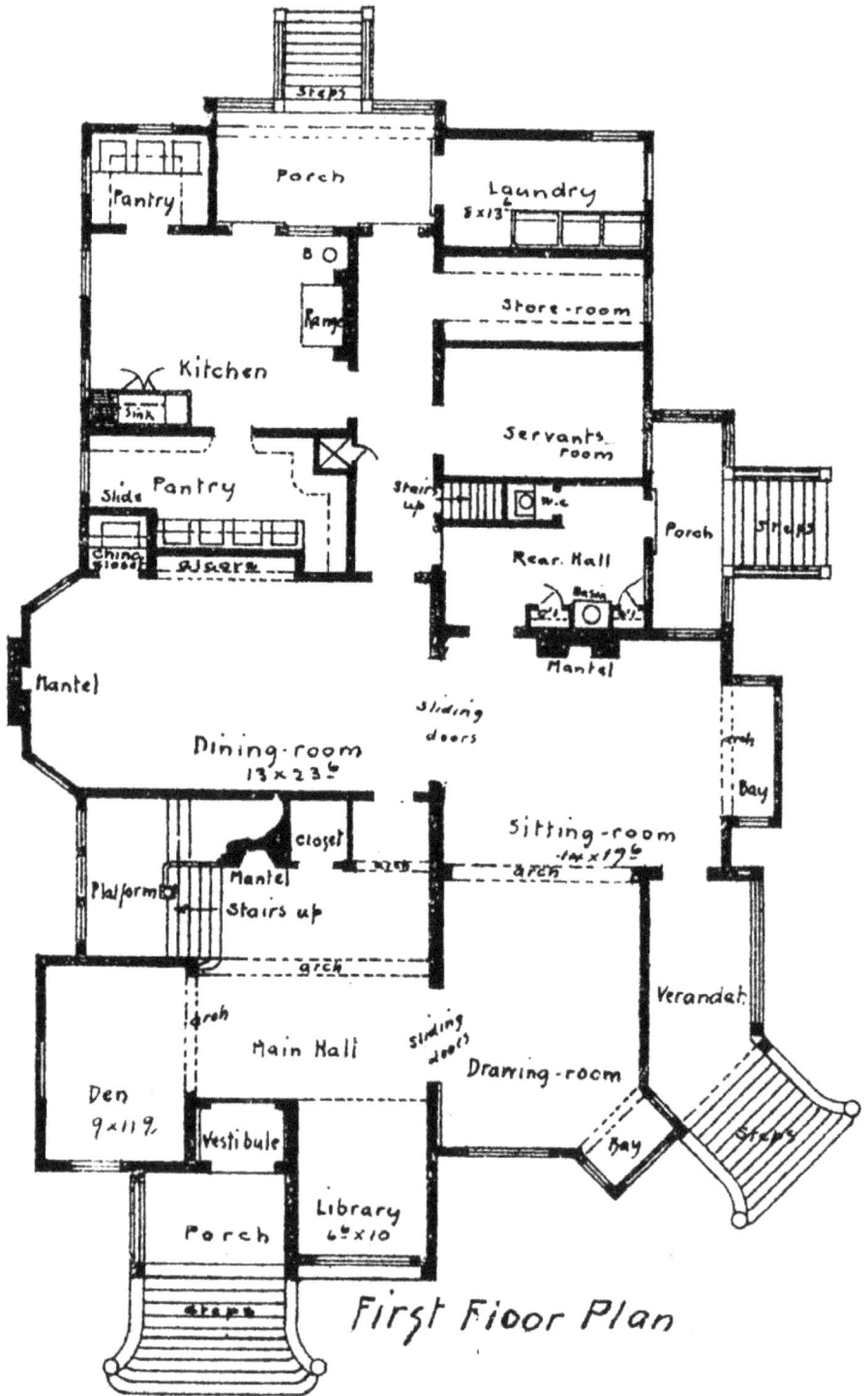

First Floor Plan

Scale   10   5   0   10   20 feet

Tub

Bath room W.C.

Chamber
12 x 14

Closet

Chamber
15 x 17

Dumb-waiter & Chute

Closet

Basin

Bath room

Closet

Basin

Basin

Closet

Tub

W.C.

Mantel

Chamber
13 x 18½

Hall

Closet

Hall
5½

Mantel

Chamber
14 x 19

Closet

Stairs down

Closet

open well

Sliding doors

alcove
8 x 16

Basin

Closet

Basin

Chamber
14 x 16

Chamber
15½ x 17½

Closet

Bay

Bal.

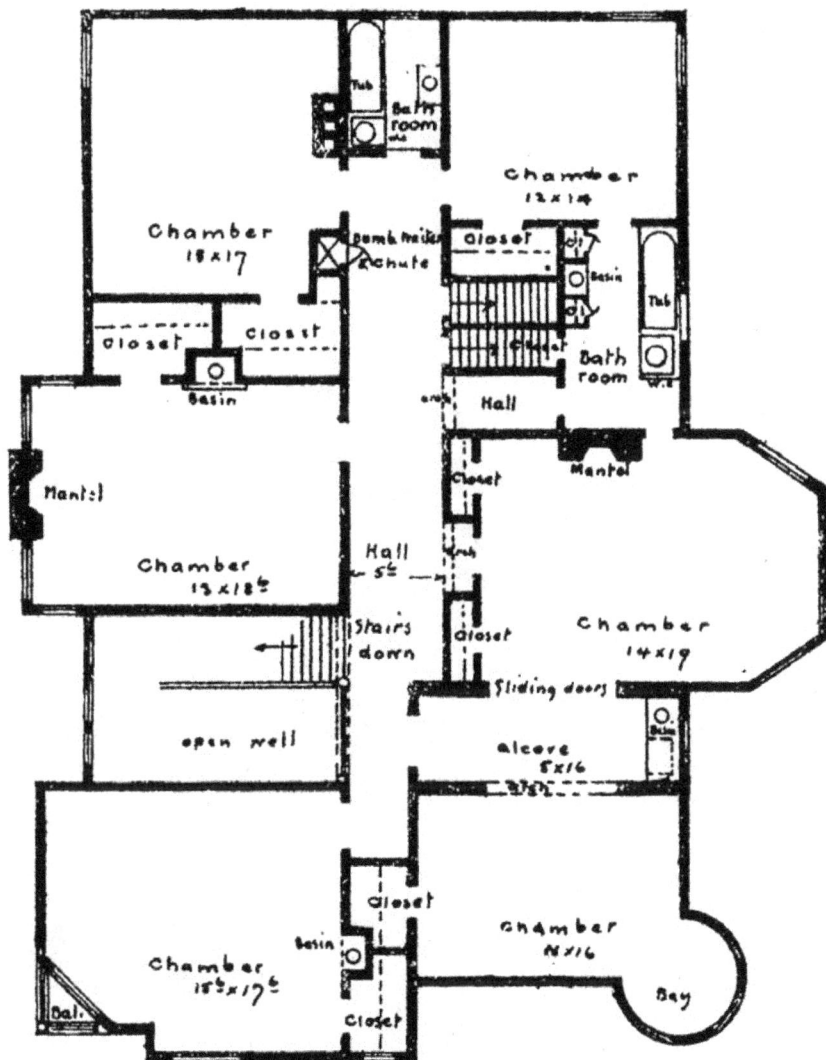

Second Floor Plan

NOB HILL.

a Dwelling in the Eastlake Style with imposing Verandah and Steep Roof with heavy projecting cornice and numerous Gables, Tower &c which make a good combination. The Main Entrance is large and Vestibule with Tile floor and rich wood work in natural finish gives a good impression at first glance. The Hall is panelled in Redwood and wood cornice and Plaster Ceiling. The Staircase is of Port Orford cedar. The Parlor, Sitting-room and Dining room are large and have Cornices and Tinted and striped. Mantels of wood. Conservatory off Dining-room. Kitchen apartments conveniently arranged in Rear. Laundry &c in Basement.
Dressing room between two front rooms

Second Floor Plan.

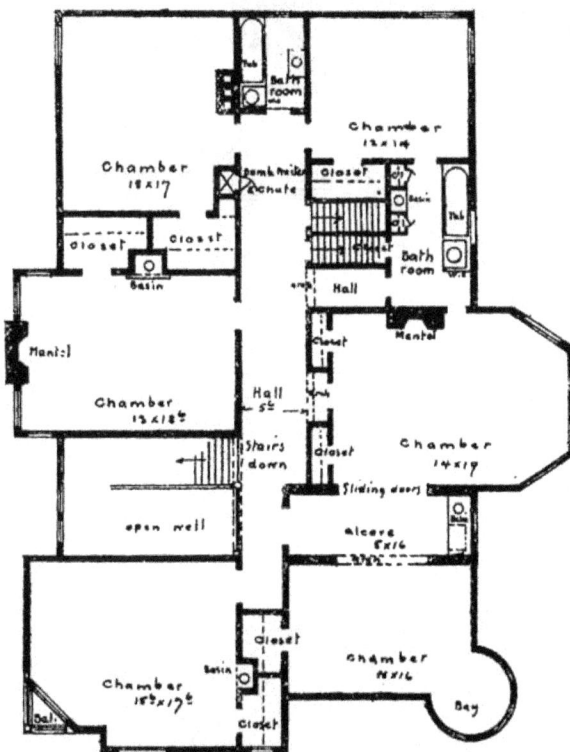

Second Floor Plan

Scale

VERNON HEIGHTS.

Estimated Cost
Lumber ———— $2500.00
Millwork ———— 3000.00
Plumbing ———— 1200.00
Plastering ———— 1025.00
Painting ———— 900.00
Labor ———— 2500.00
Hardware ———— 750.00
Iron-work ———— 800.00
Cathedral Glass— 700.00
Stairs ———— 800.00
Brickwork ———— 2800.00
Tinning———— 150.00
Wall Tinting & Lining— 700.00
Mantels———— 1000.00
Total Cost $18025.00

Parlor, Sitting-room & Dining-room con-
nected with sliding doors. Large Parlor with
Round Bay - Kitchen, Pantry, Laundry, Store
room &c in Rear
Two Bath rooms
Porch up to Belt
and Shingle
effect above mak-
posing and rich
This is in the
Knickerbocker
Style, the Stair-

Upstairs 6
large Chambers
First Story and
Course of Stone
ing a very im-
effect

case is m a convenient location. The Hall Dining
room and Library floors are of Hardwood
polished.   The Vestibule is finished in Spanish
Cedar, and presents a very rich appearance
The exterior to be painted White and Slate Roof
a quiet contrast no Blinds being used.

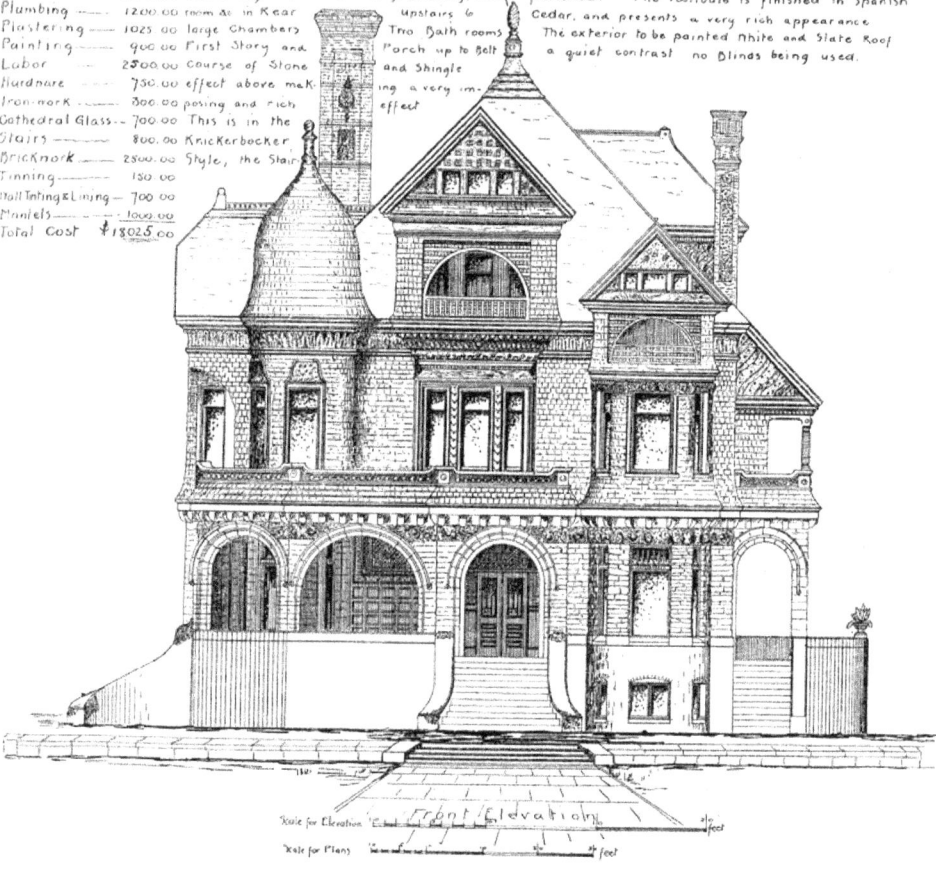

Scale for Elevation Front Elevation feet
Scale for Plans feet

Steps

Porch

Steps

Sink   Sink

Pantry

arch   Laundry
10x12

Akove   Clo.   Trays
Slide

Kitchen
11⁶x18

Pantry   Range   Boiler   Servants room
8x10
Dumb
Mantel   Waiter   Hall
Closet   Store room
16⁵x10
arch

Balcony   Dining room
16x20   Stairs
up
Sideboard   Linen   Stairs
Closet   down
Mantel   S.D.   arch   Balcony
S.D.   Hall   arch Hall   Lobby   arch
Hall   Closet
Bay   Stairs   m.c.   Porch
up
Sitting-room   arch
16x18   Cabinet   Steps
S.D.   Closet   cabinet   Mantel
Vestibule
S.D.   S.D.
Steps   Hall
arch   9x19
Library   Parlor
14⁵x16   16x27
Bay   Vestibule
arch   Bay
Verandah   Porch
arch

First Floor Plan.   Samuel & Jos. C. Newsom
Architects
504 Kearny St. (cor. California).
Steps   Top. Floor. S.F.

Store-room
10×14

Roof

Closet

Child's
n.c.

Bath
room

Dumb
waiter

Tub

Bath

Closet

Closet

Chamber
8×12 9

Stairs
up

Chamber
15×16

Hall

arch

Stairs
down

Stairs
down

Platform

Balcony

Mantel

Closet

arch

Closet

Bay

Chamber
13×20

Closet

nc

Bath-room

Pass
Closet

Closet

Closet

Hall
9×18

Chamber
12×16

Mantel

Tub

Basin
E

Balcony

Mantel

Chamber
13¼×15

arch

above

Closet

Closet

Chamber
14×16

Bay

Balcony

Bay

Balcony

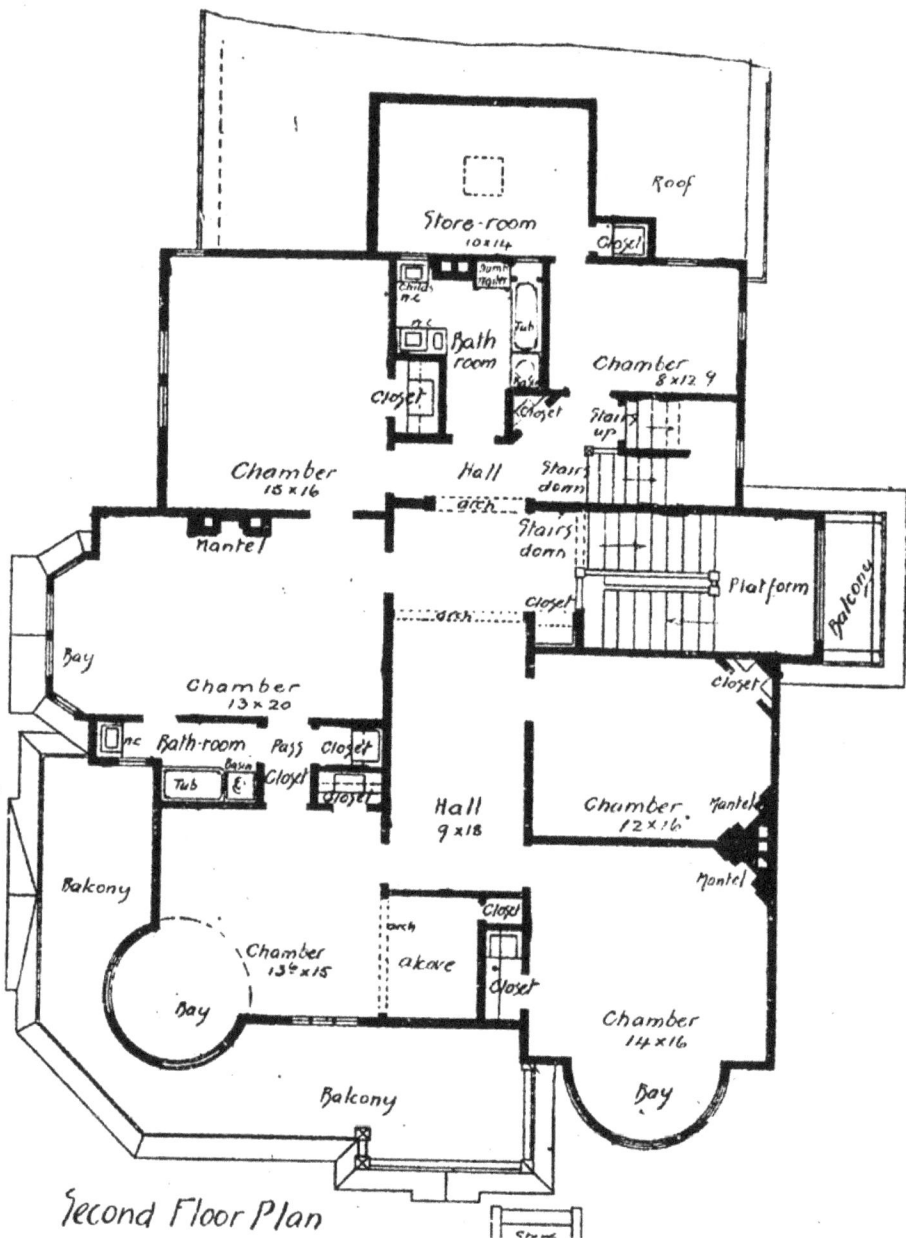

Second Floor Plan

EUREKA.

Samuel & Jos. C. Newsom
Architects
504 Kearny St
Top Floor
San Francisco.
Cal.

Scale

FRONT ELEVATION

www.ingramcontent.com/pod-product-compliance
Lightning Source LLC
Chambersburg PA
CBHW060346100426
42812CB00003B/1151